I0199737

A Timeline of Origins

A Timeline of Origins

Toward Better Integration of the Bible and Science

MICHAEL D. RUSSELL

WIPF & STOCK · Eugene, Oregon

A TIMELINE OF ORIGINS
Toward Better Integration of the Bible and Science

Wipf & Stock
An Imprint of Wipf and Stock Publishers
199 W. 8th Ave., Suite 3
Eugene, OR 97401

www.wipfandstock.com

PAPERBACK ISBN: 979-8-3852-0872-2
HARDCOVER ISBN: 979-8-3852-0873-9
EBOOK ISBN: 979-8-3852-0874-6

VERSION NUMBER 07/03/24

To Luke, Adele, Anna, and Phoebe

Contents

Acknowledgments

I AM THANKFUL TO a host of people who have contributed to the ideas in this book, its development and completion. Not long after becoming a Christian aged 17, I was wrestling with questions of science and the Bible. At that point, when I was inclined to a young-earth creationist approach, my parents made a significant specific contribution to my thinking, one of an uncountable number of excellent parenting efforts they made. Aided by longtime family friends, the Storens, they gave me a copy of Ian Plimer's *Telling Lies For God*, which, in its interaction with the Creation Science Foundation, helped me understand many of the issues at play, and the intensity of the debate.

For the training I received in problem solving, I owe thanks to Keith Hamann, Terry Tao and those from the Australian Mathematics Trust who laboured hard to teach me the skills during my youth. Specifically at the point where I was convinced the Genesis genealogies must produce a timeline, and I prayed to God for help as to how I should teach these parts of the Bible to my children, God answered the prayer through the kind of thinking I had learned in my years of Mathsearch and Maths Olympiad training.

I am thankful for the heritage of those who converted me –Richard Quadrio, Stuart Piggin and others embraced both a high view of Scripture and a mainstream view of science, and they set me on a good path in these respects. Phillip Jensen's preaching on Genesis was very important in my understanding of the book. In a compelling, well applied fashion, his preaching conveyed very well the way the promises of Genesis set the agenda for the whole Bible. I am thankful for my Hebrew and Greek teachers, including Wendy Colquhoun, Richard Gibson and Andrew Shead. I am thankful for John Woodhouse's very fine teaching of the Old Testament, with key insight into Genesis, as well as some asides from Peter Jensen, Rob Doyle and Andrew Shead that turned out to be important in bringing the ideas in this book together. There has been important input also from staff and members at St. George's Magill. Paul Hunt, Daniel Clark and Julia Zhu have all been a joy to work with, including in discussing the teaching of Genesis.

I am thankful also to those who have taught me to write, especially in long theological form. Jeff Pugh has been especially helpful in this. I am also thankful to those who have arranged and conducted the academic research seminars at the Bible College of South Australia, and thankful that they let me present material from this book multiple times as it was being developed. Graham Cole was helpful towards the end. I am thankful also to Jennifer Russell, who helped extensively with proofreading.

I am enormously thankful to God for my wife Alison, who looks after me and loves me despite my many quirks and weaknesses. It is a joy to share my life with her, and she has made her own suggestions which have shaped this book, as well as supporting me in so many other ways.

Finally, I am thankful to the God and Father of our Lord Jesus, who in his love, has given us not only a rich saving gospel, but the depths of the Scriptures to plumb, as I have sought to do here. May all the glory go to him.

Michael D. Russell

Abbreviations

BIBLICAL BOOKS

Gen	Genesis
Exod	Exodus
Num	Numbers
Deut	Deuteronomy
Josh	Joshua
Judg	Judges
1 Sam	First Samuel
Mal	Malachi
Matt	Matthew
1 Cor	First Corinthians
Gal	Galatians
Heb	Hebrews

OTHER ABBREVIATIONS

AD	Anno Domini, in the year of the Lord
ANE	Ancient Near East
BC	Before Christ
c.	*circa*, approximately
KJV	King James Version
LXX	Septuagint

MT   Masoretic Text
NIV   New International Version
y.a.   years ago

Introduction

The Perceived Clash between the Bible and Science

I HAVE A NEIGHBOR called Rob. I see him occasionally as he catches the bus, or as I walk between my house and the church I pastor. We chat. We got to the point recently of talking about Christianity, and his key objection to Christianity: that the Bible and science clash. He could not detail precisely how they clash, but his view of a clash was the main reason cited for him not being Christian.

He is not alone in this. In my home country of Australia, Mc-Crindle Research surveyed 1024 respondents in 2017. They found Christianity's stance on science and evolution blocked 34 percent from engaging with Christianity, either completely (23 percent) or significantly (11 percent).[1] No doubt there has been a shift in the cultural landscape since then, with matters of sexuality, gender, COVID-19, and war more prominent in the West, and impacting people's responses to Christianity. Nevertheless, this block to engagement regarding science and the Bible will not have disappeared in less than a decade.

The general way the Bible is seen to clash with science could be summarized in one word: evolution. But once we press for details, and ask *how* the Bible contradicts science or evolution, answers differ. So, this book will begin with the strongest version of the objection we know, so that the challenge is as clear and powerful

---

1. McCrindle, "Faith and Belief in Australia," 33.

as possible. That will be the burden of this chapter. Then in the chapters that follow, a different kind of response will be proposed, different from the ones that have been suggested for over a century since Darwin, a response centered on providing a timeline.

At the most general level, the problem has been a failure from the Christian side to provide a timeline of human history that sits comfortably with the findings of mainstream science and a high view of Scripture. To unpack this, we will consider firstly what is meant by a high view of Scripture; secondly, what is meant by the findings of mainstream science; thirdly, what is contained in the timeline derived from Genesis; and lastly, how the findings of mainstream science might contradict that timeline. The challenge will then be posed, which the remainder of the book will be devoted to addressing: we will seek to provide a timeline that aligns well with both a high view of Scripture and a mainstream view of science. We will also seek to show that our approach is at least as plausible as other approaches that maintain a high view of Scripture.

A HIGH VIEW OF SCRIPTURE

To begin then, a key assumption for this book is that of a high view of Scripture. So, the aim is to present a timeline consistent with the whole of the Bible, and not just selected parts. This in turn implies that the whole Bible is internally consistent. We will not defend that assumption in general, but only as it bears on the question of origins.

To give a reference point for this assumption, this book will operate within the "Chicago Statement on Biblical Inerrancy." That is not to promote this statement over others, nor to champion a particular expression of the Bible's inner consistency, nor to contend for inerrancy or infallibility as the best way to speak of the Bible's trustworthiness. Rather, it is a way to avoid spending unnecessary time on such details. It is chosen because this statement appears in noteworthy contributions on the subject of origins, such as that of S. Joshua Swamidass.[2]

Grounded in such a view of Scripture, this book will assume that there are claims made in the Bible, especially Genesis, that intersect with the claims of modern science, such that they need to be integrated. This is not to say that such claims are the main point of the biblical passages, nor to endorse literalistic readings of the text, but it is to say that some historical claims are made within Genesis, regarding which modern science also makes claims. It is to take a different starting point from many, including Peter Enns. For Enns wrote that "Understanding . . ." the claims of Genesis "against the backdrop of the world in which they were written, in my opinion, lays to rest any notion that these writings have any relevance to modern debates over human origins."[3] The grounds for taking a different view from Enns will become apparent as the book's argument develops, especially in chapter 5. But it should be clear at the outset that we are attempting a project that some consider misguided.

SITTING COMFORTABLY WITH THE FINDINGS OF MAINSTREAM SCIENCE

What would a theory look like if it was to sit comfortably with the findings of mainstream science? Three points are worth making. In the first place, we assume that scientific inquiry is bounded by the physical and natural world that we can observe. This means that there are claims, such as those about the nature of God, human morality, heaven, and more, that stand outside the scope of science and its findings. So, this book will present a theory with claims about such subjects. Yet it is not for that reason a book that clashes with the findings of mainstream science, since not all claims are scientific claims.

---

2. Swamidass, *Genealogical Adam*, 135.
3. Enns, *Evolution of Adam*, 33–34.

Secondly, some scientific claims, even major widely held ones, have been overturned through later theorizing and experiment, so that all scientific findings are open to correction. Yet some scientific claims are so well established, by depth of experiment and consensus in reputable sources, that a new hypothesis could not overturn those claims without significant weight of evidence and argument. In particular, we assume that it is *not* possible to propose a timeline of origins that challenges the broadly accepted methods of dating such as radiocarbon and related approaches, while still claiming to sit comfortably within the findings of mainstream science.

Yet a person could make other proposals, some aspects of which might be untestable, while sitting comfortably within the findings of mainstream science. In particular, we assume a person could advance a theory hypothesizing that *some aspects* of the human evolutionary process were miraculous in nature, involving direct intervention by God, without rendering that theory for that reason a claim outside the findings of mainstream science. We assume that a person could hypothesize that humans consist of a body *and a soul*, and that there exist worlds outside our present experience, like "Eden," without such a theory being declared, for that reason, to sit outside the findings of mainstream science.

Thirdly, there are criteria for a work to be considered a *scientific work*. A scientific work needs to provide hypotheses that are testable, and then seek to disprove those hypotheses through repeatable testing. This book will provide some hypotheses that are likely to be testable, either now or as our skill in areas like genomics improves. But this is not a scientific work; it is simply a work that aims to sit comfortably within the findings of mainstream science.

THE TIMELINE OF GENESIS

Within this high view of Scripture and mainstream understanding of science, the problem that this book will seek to solve is seen by considering the chronology that the Bible implies for its most ancient events. There has been a long history of theologians understanding that the early chapters of the Bible were written with the intent to assist construction of a timeline, all the way back to Adam. The most important data for this purpose is found in Genesis 5 and 11. For those chapters list nineteen generations of men,[4] each the son of the last, stating the age of each father at the birth of his son, sometimes called the "begetting age." This means that the numbers can be added together to produce a timeline. That is the way the genealogies were used by Jewish pre-Christ commentators,[5] early Christian commentators,[6] Augustine,[7] Calvin,[8] and Archbishop James Ussher, to name a notable few. Ussher famously calculated the date of creation as the 23rd of October, on the Julian calendar, in 4004 BC.[9] This date became famous through its publication in the marginal notes of the Authorized Version.

There are good reasons to think such a calculation is possible, in line with the intent of the book of Genesis, although not with the precision Ussher proposed. This book's appendix will outline some of the important questions in calculating key dates and explain our timeline calculations. But at this point, it is worth considering two of the main objections to such dating.

WILLIAM GREEN

The first objection came in the late nineteenth century, from William H. Green. Green's argument was expressed in greatest depth in an article entitled "Primeval Chronology," published in 1890.[10] It was termed "The Most Important Biblical Discovery of Our Time"

4. The Masoretic text differs from the Septuagint which differs from the Samaritan Pentateuch in the number of generations. These details are discussed in the appendix.

5. Merrill, "Chronology," 117–18.

6. Merrill, "Chronology," 118.

7. Augustine of Hippo, *City of God*, 1:15.12.

8. Calvin, *Genesis*, 226–27.

9. Ussher, *Annals of the World*, s. 1a.

10. Green, "Primeval Chronology," 285–303.

by one of his Princeton colleagues, professor of natural history George Macloskie.[11] After that time, his arguments steadily grew in influence, through the agency of those such as Charles Hodge,[12] B. B. Warfield, Francis Schaeffer, Old Testament scholar Ronald Youngblood, and geologist Davis Young.[13] Christian apologist William Lane Craig recently relied on Green's arguments to contend that while Genesis 1–11 has "historical interest," a timeline cannot be calculated from the genealogies.[14] So, Green's arguments remain important.

Green argued that if Matthew omits names from the ancestry of Jesus in his Gospel, which he does, Moses may have done the same in his genealogies in Genesis. If this is so, then in fact we cannot use the genealogies to determine a reliable biblical timeline, and the popular chronologies of Ussher and others may have drawn falsely on an incomplete genealogy in Genesis.

The problem with Green's argument is that even if the genealogies in Genesis were abridged, it would make no difference to the calculation of a timeline. To see this, consider the precise wording of the relevant repeated elements in the key genealogies. Genesis 5:9 says, "When Enosh had lived ninety years, he became the father of Kenan." Imagine now, with Green, that in reality Enosh was not the immediate father of Kenan, but rather a grandfather. Notice then, that if Enosh became Kenan's *grandfather*, not father, when he was ninety, then there would be the same number of years between Enosh and Kenan as there would have been were he the father, that is, still a ninety-year difference. So, making Enosh the grandfather rather than the father does not change the chronology or the timeline at all, since the difference in age remains the same. The same is true had Enosh been the great-grandfather, or any other distant ancestor.

The only way such a change would alter the chronology would be if the meaning were as follows: not that Enosh was aged

11. Numbers, "Green and Ussher," 257, 271.

12. Numbers, "Green and Ussher," 266.

13. Numbers, "Green and Ussher," 275.

14. Craig, *Historical Adam*, 143–44.

ninety when *Kenan* was born, but that Enosh was aged ninety at the time of birth of *some other person*, presumably Enosh's son, Kenan's father, in our hypothetical example. But this strains the Hebrew too far. For even though the semantic range of ילד, "beget,"[15] can include begetting grandchildren, as Green rightly points out, yet there are no clear examples in the Bible where the "begetting age" can be used in this way, with the meaning being to specify the age at birth of someone *not named*, rather than the one *actually named*. As already mentioned, Green's suggestion was made in 1890, explicitly to try to deal with the implications of Darwin's evolutionary theories, and not from any consideration stemming from the biblical text. Jeremy Sexton presents a good critique of Green's theory, including showing that it was helped at the end of the nineteenth century by an editor refusing to publish arguments against it.[16] For all these reasons, it should be seen as an unlikely reading.

QUESTIONS OF GENRE

The second significant argument against using the genealogies of Genesis for chronological purposes comes from those who dismiss the idea that Genesis as a whole, or portions of it, are intended to convey historical information. This is an objection, explicit or implied, that the genre doesn't allow for such calculation of a timeline.

Choosing just two of the expressions of such an argument, Walter Brueggemann proposed that in the entire book of Genesis, Israel passes on a faith, not "a structure of reality (as in myth), nor a chronicle of events (as in history). Rather, it is about a memory that is transformed, criticized and extended each time it is told."[17] So, for Brueggemann, Genesis's genre is such that history is not intended to be conveyed through it, and so a historical timeline was not intended to be constructed from its contents.

---

15. Hifil stem.
16. Sexton, "Chronological Gaps," 11–12.
17. Brueggemann, *Genesis*, 4.

Daniel Lowery, on the other hand, through his detailed study of Gen 4:17–22, argued that Genesis 1–11, including its genealogies, may be characterized as a "poetics of protohistory."[18] So, Lowery did not deny that actual events are being described, but did make it clear that the genealogies should not be used for chronological purposes.[19]

Such are two of many top-down dismissals of the notion that Genesis might be communicating history, making them also top-down dismissals of the notion that the genealogical data can be used to construct a timeline. Such dismissals, grounded as they are in disputes about Genesis's genre, are best answered in bottom-up fashion. That is, we will understand best how the genealogical data is intended to be read by looking at details of how this specific data is actually used in Genesis and beyond. The following four considerations are noteworthy:

Firstly, the lengthy lifespans of Genesis 5 and 11 continue into Genesis 12–50. After the flood, lifespans of the descendants of Adam decline exponentially, from the typical nine-hundred-year pre-flood expectation toward modern-day normality. But this transition plays out well after the conclusion of Genesis 11. So, in Gen 25:7 we are told that "Abraham lived a hundred and seventy-five years." In Gen 35:28, we are told that "Isaac lived a hundred and eighty years." In Deuteronomy, we read, "Moses was a hundred and twenty years old when he died, yet his eyes were not weak nor his strength gone."[20] Thus, it is untenable to claim that Genesis 1–11 depicts "unhistorical" or "unrealistic" lifespans, while Genesis 12 and following depict historical, realistic lifespans. Rather, specifically regarding the lifespan data, the transition is a smooth one, after the flood, across all of Genesis and beyond.

Most significant in this regard is the narrative of Gen 47:9: "And Jacob said to Pharaoh, 'The years of my pilgrimage are a hundred and thirty. My years have been few and difficult, and they do not equal the years of the pilgrimage of my fathers.'" That is, the

18. Lowery, *Poetics of Genesis 1–11*, 237.
19. Lowery, *Poetics of Genesis 1–11*, 239.
20. Deut 34:7.

Genesis narrative has on the lips of Jacob an acknowledgement that his 130 years had been fewer and more difficult than his ancestors. So, even in the midst of a section that is depicting historical narrative, the text implies that Jacob's ancestors, including those listed in Genesis 5 and 11, lived lives extraordinary in length and in ease, by our "normal" standards. That is, this narrative in Genesis 47 points to the fact that the length of years stated in those early chapters is meant to be taken at face value.

The second consideration to confirm us in the use of genealogies for chronological purposes is this: that it should not be considered a coincidence that Genesis gives precisely the data required to produce a timeline. If the intent had been to convey only the longevity of the patriarchs, then the author or final editor did not need to provide the age of each father at their son's birth in Gen 5:1–32; 11:10–26; 21:5; or 25:26. That this specific data is provided repeatedly, not just in the genealogies, but in the later narrative, points to the purpose being to allow a timeline to be constructed. If the Genesis author did not want us to create a timeline using the age data, it is unlikely that such pains would have been made to give us exactly the data needed to produce one.

The third consideration is this: that no plausible alternative has been given as to the choice of particular lifespans through the book of Genesis. That is, the obvious and clear reading is that Genesis depicts these long lifespans to recount the actual years lived by each of these men, and the actual age they were at the birth of their respective sons. Those who are unwilling to accept this reading commonly suggest that some kind of symbolism might be used, for example pointing to the 777 years attributed to Lamech by the Masoretic text of Genesis 5:31.[21] In his Genesis commentary, Gordon Wenham was right, and still is, in his rebuttal and conclusion: "To date, then, no writer has offered an adequate explanation of these figures. If they are symbolic, it is not clear what they

---

21. The Septuagint has 753 years for Lamech. Such discrepancies are discussed in the appendix.

symbolize. If they are to be taken literally, we are left with the historical problems with which we began."[22]

Put another way, if we do not want to say the author invented these ages randomly, and we do not want to say he intended to convey actual lifespans, then the best explanation is that the numbers are symbolic in some way. But there is no symbolism to be found that explains all the numbers. So, it is best to conclude that the numbers are meant to convey actual lifespans, which could therefore be used to calculate a timeline.

The fourth consideration is a comment regarding the *default position* for those who might be coming to this question for the first time. Recall that the overwhelming consensus until the time of Charles Darwin was that the relevant ages of the men in Genesis 5 and 11 could be added together to produce a timeline. Those who held such views, such as Jewish pre-Christ commentators, early Christian commentators, Augustine, Calvin, and many more, include many who were not ignorant of the relevance of genre to such a question. Therefore, given that the change in viewpoint on this question was driven primarily by evolutionary considerations outside of the Bible, rather than from considerations within the biblical text, we may conclude that the burden of proof still sits with those who would deny that these genealogies should be used for a timeline, rather than those who would affirm it. The position advocated here, then, can rightly be seen as the default position for those with a high view of Scripture coming to this question afresh.

Whatever the conclusion made about the genre of these sections of Genesis then, these four points are best taken as decisive on the question of timeline, since they are directly and specifically pertinent to the question. They are more pertinent than Lowery's study on Gen 4:17–22,[23] since the genealogies described there have no attached age data. Indeed, these four points ought to contribute

---

22. Wenham, *Genesis 1–15*, 134.

23. Note that Craig incisively critiqued an influential study by Robert Wilson on the historical interest of genealogies, by pointing out the flaws in his narrow focus on the genealogy of Gen 4:17–22. See Craig, *Historical Adam*, 140–42; Wilson, *Genealogy and History*, 154, 166.

to the discussion of genre in bottom-up fashion, rather than being overridden by top-down genre considerations.

But as Wenham wrote, this in turn gives us significant historical problems. That is, we must now face the problem of how the timeline implied by the Genesis genealogies might fit with the findings of mainstream science and history.

THE FINDINGS OF MAINSTREAM SCIENCE AND HISTORY

The specific calculations of the relevant dates are left to the appendix. But, with textual variants alone meaning these dates may be too early by up to 1550 years for Adam and 950 years for the flood, Genesis implies the following: a date for Adam and Eve around 5100 BC, for the great flood around 2900 BC, and for the scattering at Babel around 2370–2030 BC. Even given this size of potential error, these dates are sufficient to produce significant problems, in terms of integrating such a timeline with what we know from mainstream science and history. Just some of the problems are as follows.

Firstly, significant problems arise if the great flood is taken to have destroyed all humans except Noah's family in 2900 BC. Just one specific problem is that we have examples of written material in Egypt, existing continuously through time, as far back as the accounting tags found in King Scorpion I's tomb, before 2900 BC.[24] One can ask how such an unbroken set of written material could exist through the time of the flood if all people were wiped out in that flood.

Secondly, there are objections to a truly global flood that have force irrespective of the purported timing. So, one could ask about the amount of water required to cover Mt. Everest, or even the mountains of Ararat for that matter, known to the writer of Genesis. One could ask where the water came from and where it went afterwards. It is also worth quoting Richard Dawkins, who made a strong critique about the distribution of animals after the flood,

---

24. King Scorpion I's tomb dates to between 3400 and 3200 BC. See Mattessich, "Oldest Writings," 195–97.

which is powerful if the claim is that the ancestors of all modern animals stepped off an ark in modern-day Turkey, no matter when that is claimed to have occurred:

> Why would all those marsupials—ranging from tiny pouched mice through koalas and bilbys to giant kangaroos and Diprotodonts—why would all those marsupials, but no placentals at all, have migrated en masse from Mount Ararat to Australia? Which route did they take? And why did not a single member of their straggling caravan pause on the way, and settle—in India, perhaps, or China, or some haven along the Great Silk Road?[25]

The objection is that the distribution of marsupials globally is not consistent with the thesis that ancestors of all modern animals were together in an ark that landed in Turkey. This objection is potent if the claim is that the flood destroyed all land animals. But it is more potent still if we date the flood as recently as 2900 BC, since after that time there has been no land bridge to assist all the marsupials in making the trip to Australia. If, on the other hand, we limit our understanding of the flood's extent to some localized area in Turkey, we can ask why God needed to save all those animals if some members of their species were going to survive elsewhere, outside the bounds of the flood. After all, one of the purposes of taking the animals into the ark was "to keep their various kinds alive throughout the earth."[26]

Thirdly, turning to the humans on the ark, the problems are significant if we want to say all humans are biologically descended from Noah in 2900 BC, or even from Adam and Eve in 5100 BC. For if we say that, we must contradict mainstream findings around the dates of human arrival in Australia, the Americas, and elsewhere. For the mainstream view is that biological humans arrived in those locations well before 5100 BC.[27]

Fourthly, there is the question of the development of human languages. If we take Genesis 11 to mean that the first human

25. Dawkins, *Greatest Show*, 268.

26. Gen 7:3.

27. Clarkson et al., "Human Occupation of Australia," 306–10.

language was confused at Babel in c. 2370–2030 BC, how then do we have records of multiple written languages before that time, the Sumerian texts and the Old Egyptian hieroglyphic texts being noteworthy examples. Or, from a different angle, how can we understand the meaning of the Babel event if we say that it occurred in 2370–2030 BC and we also say, with the mainstream scientific consensus, that in various places like Australia people were speaking a great array of languages in 2370 BC, quite different in character from those spoken in Mesopotamia at the same time? This seems irreconcilable with the claim of Gen 11:9 that at Babel "the Lord confused the language of the whole world."

A fifth aspect of the problem is how one might explain the fine cave art and portable art that mainstream science dates to well before 5100 BC, and credits to teams rather than individuals.[28] One can ask whether it is viable to credit all these achievements in cave art and the like to a species of prehuman beings. Or instead, will the defender of the Genesis chronology seek to undermine all the science that is used to date such ancient specimens?

CONCLUSION

In an introduction, it is wise not to overdo the details. This should be enough for the scale of the problem to be clear. What have we seen in this chapter? We have seen that the impression of a clash between the Bible and science is responsible for many rejecting Christianity. We have seen reasons for this perceived clash: that when one takes a high view of Scripture, the best conclusion is that the early parts of the Bible convey a timeline of human origins. We have seen that this timeline seems to clash fundamentally with modern understandings of science, evolution, and history, and that it is hard to see how this clash might be resolved.

The next chapter will respond to this challenge by presenting an original timeline that seeks to integrate this chronology from Genesis with the findings of mainstream science and history. The

28. Tattersall, *Becoming Human*, 18–28, 178.

chapters that follow will then seek to defend the timeline in more detail, arguing not only that it is plausible biblically and scientifically, but also that it is at least as plausible as other approaches that hold to a high view of Scripture.

Chapter 1

Understanding the Timeline

INTRODUCTION

THE PURPOSE OF THIS chapter is to present the centerpiece of this book: the proposed timeline. The easiest way to understand this book is to read and understand the timeline. So, this chapter will consist of the timeline first, then some explanations necessary to understand it, and finally an examination of one key passage relevant to the discussion, 2 Pet 3:5–7. Here, then, is our proposal for a way forward for those holding a high view of Scripture and wishing to sit within the findings of mainstream science.

THE TIMELINE

Date	"The Present Heavens and Earth" (2 Pet 3:7) "The Twice-Cursed World." The World We Live in—Our Physical World	"The World of That Time" (2 Pet 3:6) "The Once-Cursed World." The World of Adam through Noah
c. 4.5 billion years ago	"The Present Earth" was formed around 4.5 billion years ago.[1]	There were no humans, either mere "biological humans" or "theological humans" fully in God's image, or any animals of any sort, in "the world of that time" until around 5100 BC.
c. 65,000 years ago	The ancestors of in-digenous Australians arrived in the combined Pleistocene landmass of Australia and New Guinea around 65,000 years ago.[2]	
c. 35,000 years ago	The earliest examples of sophisticated cave art are dated to around 35,000 years ago, in Europe.[3]	

1. Dalrymple, "Age of the Earth," 205–21.
2. Clarkson et al., "Human Occupation of Australia," 306–10.
3. Humphrey and Stringer, *Our Human Story*, 84.

Date	"The Present Heavens and Earth" (2 Pet 3:7) "The Twice-Cursed World." The World We Live in—Our Physical World	"The World of That Time" (2 Pet 3:6) "The Once-Cursed World." The World of Adam through Noah
Best estimate for Adam's creation: c. 5100 BC Plausible Range for Adam's creation: c. 5600–3700 BC	While there were "biological humans" all over the world before Adam's sin, there were still no full humans until that event. There were "biological humans" that looked like us, but they did not act like us fully, for they had not yet been given human souls—they were not "theological humans" in the image of God before c. 5100 BC.	Adam and Eve were created, the first full humans in God's image in any world. They likely spoke Sumerian, the sole language of "the world of that time." They had the first marriage; c. 5100 BC (Gen 2:4–25; 11:1). God created and brought the animals to Adam for naming. There were no ugly, dangerous, or diseased animals. There were no earthquakes, no sunburn, etc. It was paradise; c. 5100 BC.
Best estimate for the fall: c. 5100 BC Plausible range for the fall: c. 5600–3700 BC	After Adam's creation and fall, all the "biological humans" in our world were made fully human. What was still lacking in their humanity was now supplied by God, modeled on Adam's humanity, so that they all became fully human, in God's image.	Adam sinned. The ground was cursed, so this world became "the once-cursed world." Yet God promised that Eve's descendant would crush the serpent's head, that is, that one day, Jesus would crush Satan (Gen 3); c. 5100 BC. Adam and Eve were expelled from the garden, and from the tree of life. But they did not leave "the once-cursed world"; c. 5100 BC (Gen 3:20–24).

Date	"The Present Heavens and Earth" (2 Pet 3:7) "The Twice-Cursed World." The World We Live in—Our Physical World	"The World of That Time" (2 Pet 3:6) "The Once-Cursed World." The World of Adam through Noah
Best estimate range for Cain's descendants' growing influence before the flood: c. 5000–2900 BC Widest plausible range: 5600–2050 BC	Cain arrived in our world, expelled from the ancient "once-cursed world" into our "twice-cursed world." He married and built a city. His descendants were pioneers in tent-making, livestock, and music. His lifespan was longer than those around him; c. 5000 BC (Gen 4:17–24). His language, likely Sumerian, was not spoken in our world until his arrival, c. 5000 BC. Cain's descendants flourished and had significant influence; c. 5000–2900 BC (Gen 4:10–24).	Cain killed Abel, and was expelled from "the once-cursed world" as punishment; c. 5000 BC (Gen 4:2–16). Adam's descendants consistently lived to over 900 years of age in "the world of that time"; c. 5000—c. 2900 BC (Gen 5; 11:10–26).
Best estimate for the flood: c. 2900 BC Plausible range for the flood: c. 3300–2050 BC	The nations steadily spread out across the world through the clans of the sons of Noah; c. 2900 BC–present day (Genesis 10).	The great flood destroyed "the world of that time" in entirety; c. 2900 BC (Gen 6–8). "The world of that time" became a wasteland. All that remained were the spirits of those who had died; c. 2900 BC–present day.

Date	"The Present Heavens and Earth" (2 Pet 3:7) "The Twice-Cursed World." The World We Live in—Our Physical World	"The World of That Time" (2 Pet 3:6) "The Once-Cursed World." The World of Adam through Noah
Best estimate for "the time of Peleg": c. 2370–2030 BC Widest plausible range: 2780–1720 BC	The Babel scattering occurred. The Sumerian-speaking people and their language were dispersed. The Tower of Babel was one of the Mesopotamian "ziggurats"; c. 2370–2030 BC (Gen 11:1–9).	
Best estimate for the exodus: c. 1270 BC Plausible alternatives: 1446 BC / c. 1270 BC	The exodus; c. 1270 BC	
586 BC	The fall of Jerusalem; 586 BC	
Best estimate for Jesus' birth: 4 BC Most likely range: 6–4 BC	The birth of Jesus; 4 BC	
30/33 AD	The death and resurrection of Jesus; 30/33 AD	After his death, before his resurrection, Jesus travelled in the Spirit to "the world of that time." He proclaimed his victory to the spirits of those who had died long before; 30/33 AD (1 Pet 3:19–20).
30/33 AD–present	The gospel of Jesus will be preached to all nations, the preaching having started in Jerusalem (Luke 24:44–49).	

At least four clarifications are helpful to explain this timeline, three of which will be made in this chapter, and one of which will wait for chapter 2. Firstly, it is useful to clarify the terminology around the word "human," especially the distinction between "biological humans," "mere biological humans," and "theological humans," which this book will sometimes call "full humans." Secondly, it is useful to explain the nature of the distinction between the second and third column of the timeline, that is, the distinction between "the world of that time" and the "present heavens and earth." Thirdly, it will be argued in this chapter that the nature of the language in 2 Pet 3:5–7 not only makes it possible to distinguish two physical worlds, as this timeline does, but makes such a distinction likely. Fourthly, the alternate headings for the second and third columns, "the twice-cursed world" and "the once-ucrsed world," need to be explained, for which, see chapter 2.

DEFINING "HUMAN"

In 2011, the Catholic philosopher Kenneth Kemp suggested the use of three parallel definitions of "human": the biological, the philosophical, and the theological.[4] For Kemp, the biological species is "the population of interbreeding individuals."[5] The philosophical species is "the rational animal, i.e., a natural kind characterized by the capacity for conceptual thought, judgment, reasoning and free choice."[6] The theological species is "the collection of individuals that have an eternal destiny," those in God's image.[7]

The need for the distinction between theological and biological species arises for those who, like Kemp and this book, want to propose that there were humans outside the garden of Eden, who had biological ancestors dating from before the time of Adam. This implies that there is not a complete overlap between the theological and biological human historically, hence the need for the distinction. That is, if we assume there were some human-looking beings in the distant past, which had not yet been given a human soul by God,

4. Kemp, "Science, Theology and Monogenesis," 230.

5. Kemp, "Science, Theology and Monogenesis," 230.

6. Kemp, "Science, Theology and Monogenesis," 230.

7. Kemp, "Science, Theology and Monogenesis," 230.

we need a way to describe their humanity and distinguish it from ours. Kemp's definitions allow space to do this. Thus, Kemp has provided terminology through which we can speak of ancient biological humans, who were at some point "made" into a new theological species by "being given a rational soul and an eternal destiny."[8]

Kemp's *threefold* definition is, however, unnecessary for our purposes. There are some who might like to argue that before Adam, some "biological humans" also had rational abilities equal to modern humans, without being fully human. They might characterise such a being using the term "philosophical human," in line with Kemp. For this book, such terminology will not be used. Indeed, it will be argued in due course that the viewpoint that gives rise to such terminology has problems.

Our approach, then, will be more like that of Swamidass, who considered a twofold definition sufficient for his discussion.[9] We define the "theological human" as a being with all the faculties, endowments, and appointments, physical and otherwise, required for the person to be in God's image. For brevity, such theological humans will sometimes be referred to as "full humans" or just "humans." The "biological human," on the other hand, is defined as the "anatomically modern human," a term that often appears in scientific literature. This term refers to a being that may or may not have received a human soul to make them theologically human, but certainly has the physical characteristics to qualify as biologically human, being a member of the species *Homo sapiens*. The term "mere biological human" will be used to specify that the biological human in question *does not* have a human soul, but is *merely* a biological human. The biblical validity for a term referring specifically to the biological aspect of our humanity can be grounded in the biblical use of the word "body," as distinguished from "soul," or "soul" and "spirit," in such places as Matt 10:28 and 1 Thess 5:13.

---

8. Kemp, "Science, Theology and Monogenesis," 231.

9. Swamidass distinguishes biological and "textual" humans, where the text he has in mind is the biblical text. See Swamidass, *Genealogical Adam*, 133–34.

THE DISTINCTION BETWEEN TWO WORLDS

Even more important in understanding the timeline is to grasp the distinction made by separating the second and third columns. That is, it is important to explain the distinction between the column labeled "the present heavens and earth" and the column labeled "the world of that time." Notice first that quotation marks punctuate those two labels, because the distinction in worlds is grounded in the words of 2 Pet 3:5–7. Here is that section of Peter's letter, with the two phrases marked by italics:

> But they deliberately forget that long ago by God's word the heavens came into being and the earth was formed out of water and by water. By these waters also *the world of that time* was deluged and destroyed. By the same word *the present heavens and earth* are reserved for fire, being kept for the day of judgment and destruction of the ungodly.[10]

It is critical to the timeline above that the distinction in this passage be made between two different *physical* worlds. That is, when the world of that time was destroyed by the great flood, the present heavens and earth were not. Put another way, it is critical to this book's proposal that Peter's words *could be read* such that the world of that time was flooded and destroyed, without our present world suffering the same fate.

This is not as strange an understanding as it may first seem. When pressed, many Christians will admit that they do not think the garden of Eden is, or was, in our world. They will say that they think Eden is in another place, without being able to specify its current or past location. Wenham is an example of a commentator open to that possibility. He wrote, "Maybe the reversed flow of the rivers" in Eden "suggests that paradise is beyond man's present experience." The names of the rivers mentioned in Gen 2:10–14 "affirm that there was a garden there, but maybe the insoluble

---

10. 2 Pet 3:5–7, emphasis mine.

geography is a way of saying that it is now inaccessible to, even unlocatable by, later man."[11]

What is being proposed then is to take that kernel of an idea and to press it further. We propose that this first paradise was in another place, unlocatable by later man and beyond our present experience. The proposal is that it was a real physical place, since the New Testament teaches that Adam was a real physical person. Further, we propose that it was a different physical world from ours, since the perfection of such a paradise is not possible anywhere in our world of earthquakes, viruses, and lightning strikes. But it was not just Adam and Eve who inhabited an unlocatable place beyond our present experience. Rather, we propose that all of the ancient patriarchs, from Adam through to Noah, lived in a different physical world to ours. So, the whole account of Gen 2:4—4:10 and 4:25—8:9 is set in this other world.

We further hypothesize that there were two crossings made between the world of that time and ours, crossings described in Genesis. These crossings could be labelled as "miraculous," or as occurring by God's special intervention. The first is the eviction of Cain from that world to ours, explicitly mentioned in Gen 4:11–14 with implications described and explained in 4:15–24. The second is the miraculous translation of the ark of Noah from that world to ours, the miracle implied by the word הִנֵּה, "behold" in Gen 8:11. Implications of the "translation" of the ark into our world are spelt out in Gen 8:16—9:18.

Can 2 Pet 3:5–7 be read consistently with such an understanding? We now turn to consider whether this key passage might not only *allow* such a reading, but even contain elements that *favor* such a reading of it.

2 PETER 3:5-7

In 2 Pet 3:6 the participle κατακλυσθεὶς, "having been deluged," governs the main verb ἀπώλετο, "was destroyed," so that the last

---

11. Wenham, *Genesis 1–15*, 66–67.

part of the verse literally reads, "the world of that time, having been deluged, was destroyed." Notice that the notion of "deluge" is already enough to communicate that the people were killed and that there was significant damage done to the physical world. This means that the further addition of the verb ἀπώλετο, "was destroyed," serves to underscore the complete demolition of the physical world. Peter's phrasing, then, is at least suggestive of the idea that the physical world of that time might have been destroyed such that further habitation was impossible.

Commentators, when discussing this phrasing, have focused energy on the question of whether Peter is teaching that the heavens were destroyed.[12] Richard Bauckham, for example, supported such a view, by referring to Genesis 7:

> 'This idea', that the heavens were destroyed in the flood, 'is not so alien to the Genesis narrative as many commentators allege: according to Gen 7:11 the waters of chaos, confined at the creation above the firmament, poured through the windows of the firmament to inundate the earth.'[13]

That is, Bauckham's understanding was not just that the flood inundated the ground for a while and killed the people, and that was it. Bauckham argued that Peter saw permanent damage done to the actual heavens in the manner of the flood. He based that understanding on Genesis's description of the destruction of the firmament in the sky by the waters of the great flood. But if we are able, with Bauckham, to see such destruction of the heavens implied in Peter's verb ἀπώλετο, "was destroyed," we should also be able to see in his words the destruction of the rest of the physical world of that time. After all, the subject of that verb ἀπώλετο, "was destroyed," is not just the heavens but the whole τότε κόσμος, "world of that time." This book is open to the possibility that the world of that time might have been so different in physical makeup to our own that it had a physical firmament in the sky holding up

12. Green comments on the "heavy weather" commentators have made of this discussion. Green, *Second Peter & Jude*, 142.

13. Bauckham, *Jude, 2 Peter*, 299.

torrents of water, until those waters broke through and destroyed that world.

A final point from this passage is relevant. Consider again the distinction between worlds that Peter makes: He contrasts "the world of that time," ὁ τοτε κοσμος, literally "the then world," with "the present heavens and earth," ὁι . . . νυν οὐρανοι καὶ ἡ γη, literally "the now heavens and earth." Thus, if "the then world" refers to the same world as the one we live in, there should be no need to describe our universe as "the *present* heavens and earth," for no other heavens and earth would ever have existed. So, the fact that Peter does speak of "the *present* heavens and earth" makes it more likely that he is implying the existence of two *distinct* physical universes—"the present heavens and earth," on the one hand, and "the world of that time," on the other hand.

So, these three points support the plausibility, if not the likelihood, that 2 Pet 3:5–7 speaks of two physically distinct places, "the present heavens and earth" as distinct from "the world of that time": Firstly, the use of the participle as well as the verb, "having been deluged, was destroyed," supports a complete destruction of that world. Secondly, the fact that Genesis 7 plausibly describes the great flood permanently destroying the heavens supports the notion that Peter might be implying permanent destruction of the whole "world of that time" in 2 Pet 3:6. Thirdly, the distinction between "the *now* heavens and the earth" and "the world *of that time*" points to physically distinct worlds.

CONCLUSION

This chapter began with the timeline this book is proposing, which is its centerpiece. It continued by explaining two elements which are key to understand the timeline. The first was the terminology regarding the human species. So, a differentiation was made between the "biological human," the "mere biological human," and the full "theological human," the first not necessarily possessing more than modern human anatomy, the second not possessing more, and the third possessing all that goes with being in the image of God.

The second element necessary to understand the timeline was the nature of the distinction between the two rightmost columns in the timeline, namely the distinction between "the world of that time" and "the present heavens and earth." It was explained that the terminology comes directly from 2 Pet 3:5–7, and hinges on the understanding that two physically distinct worlds are meant by those phrases. This was seen not to be as far-fetched as some might think, given other common understandings of the location of the garden of Eden place it outside of this physical world. It was argued from the phrasing of 2 Pet 3:6, "having been deluged was destroyed," that such an understanding of the text was not only possible, but favored.

So, with the timeline presented, and some elements of its plausibility defended, we turn in the next chapter to consider biblical arguments for and against there being people from outside the garden at the time of Cain's banishment. For the existence of such people is an essential element of the timeline here presented, and is contested among those who take a high view of Scripture.

Chapter 2

People from Outside the Garden
To Where Was Cain Banished?

INTRODUCTION

THE OPENING CHAPTER OUTLINED the problem this book is addressing: the perceived clash between the Bible and science. It indicated that this book would attempt to resolve that perceived clash by providing a timeline of origins consistent with both a high view of Scripture and a mainstream view of science. Chapter 1 presented that timeline, as the centerpiece of this book. It then expanded on aspects of it, and explained the differentiation between the key terms "theological human," "biological human," and "mere biological human." It also explained and defended the notion that the Bible depicts two physically different worlds, one having been destroyed at the flood, and the other being the world we live in today.

This chapter will center on a claim that must be true, if that timeline is to be accepted: the claim is that there were "people from outside the garden."[1] The word "from" in that phrase should

---

1. The claim slightly adjusts the phrase from S. Joshua Swamidass, who argued that there were "people outside the garden of Eden." So important is that claim for Swamidass's book that 67 pages out of a book of 241 discuss "people outside the garden," according to the general index. See Swamidass,

be understood not in terms of the homeland of these individuals, but in terms of their ancestry. The question in mind is whether all people are biologically sourced from Adam and Eve and the garden, that is, universally descended entirely from them, or whether some people have their ancestry partly sourced elsewhere. Our argument is that the latter is plausibly consistent with the teaching of the Bible.

The main argument of the chapter then is this: that it is consistent with a high view of Scripture to say that there were people from outside the garden. Or, put another way, that it is consistent with Scripture to say that at the time of Cain's banishment, there were already full theological humans, who were not his relatives, in the place where Cain was banished. This will be argued in three ways. Firstly, we will argue that this conclusion is likely when considering the narrative of Genesis 4 in isolation, where a distinction can be made between the "twice-cursed land" of Cain's banishment and the "once-cursed land" he left behind. Secondly and thirdly, we will consider two sections of Scripture that many take to refute this conclusion, namely Gen 3:20 and Acts 17:26. This chapter will present understandings of these passages that are consistent with the book's timeline, and consistent with the notion that there are people from outside the garden.

PEOPLE FROM OUTSIDE THE GARDEN: THE SUPPORT FROM GENESIS 4

Expanding on the analysis of Swamidass, the following observations support the conclusion that Genesis 4 implies the existence of people from outside the garden:[2]

The first observation regards Cain's fear. When Cain was exiled to the land of Nod for murdering his brother Abel,[3] he said, "I will be a restless wanderer on the earth, and whoever finds me will

---

Genealogical Adam, 245–46.

    2. Swamidass, *Genealogical Adam*, 143–44.

    3. Gen 4:10–16.

kill me."[4] God placed a mark on Cain in response to his fear, which endorsed that fear as legitimate and enduring.[5] But whom did he fear? The answer is that he feared people in the land of Nod.[6] We suggest that those were people from outside the garden.

The alternative is that he was afraid of an attack from his relatives, at the time of his banishment or later. This might have been from Adam and Eve or unmentioned contemporary siblings in the short term. Or it might have been from a yet-unborn relative. This fear could have been derived from the concern that his relatives might, perhaps many years hence, go to Nod and kill him, in retribution for Abel. But this is unlikely for a few reasons.

Firstly, to do this, they, like Cain, would have to leave the אֲדָמָה, "land" or "ground,"[7] and so be hidden from God's "presence"[8] like Cain had been. Cain was so disturbed by this thought that he called it a "punishment," "more than I can bear."[9] Moreover, Gen 4:11a could be literally translated, "Now you are cursed away from the land." That is, with Wenham, we can understand that a central part of the curse on Cain *consists* in his banishment.[10] This makes the idea of going from the "land" of Adam and Eve to the "land" of Cain's punishment a sufficiently negative experience that we should doubt his family would have pursued him due to the high personal cost.

More than that, the phrase גֵּרַשְׁתָּ אֹתִי הַיּוֹם מֵעַל פְּנֵי הָאֲדָמָה, "today you are driving me from the land," in Gen 4:14, looks to imply that he could not return from his place of punishment to the land of his birth, because he had been banished irreversibly. This is reinforced by the use of repeated language between Genesis 3 and 4: important repeated vocabulary between those chapters includes ארור, "cursed," אדמה, "land," and especially גרש, "drive,"

4. Gen 4:14.
5. Gen 4:15.
6. Gen 4:16.
7. Gen 4:13.
8. Gen 4:14.
9. Gen 4:13.
10. See Wenham, *Genesis 1–15*, 107.

the latter found in both Gen 3:24 and 4:14.[11] Given that Adam and Eve were banished permanently from the garden of Eden, we can reasonably infer, using these parallels, that Cain's banishment was also permanent. The permanency of the mark[12] placed on him by God also speaks to a permanent separation of Cain from the land of his parents. But if Cain was permanently cut off from the land of Adam and Eve, it seems likely that his parents were also permanently cut off from him. In this case, the people Cain feared in Nod could not have been those who might travel to him from the land of Adam and Eve, for such travel would not be possible.

Cain was told by God, "When you work the ground, it will no longer yield its crops for you." It is logically possible that this meant that God would make sure anything Cain did by way of farming would be less successful than similar work done by anyone else. But such repeated special intervention by God seems less likely than the conclusion that the whole of the land of Cain's banishment was worse for farming than the land he was banished from. This is especially so if we accept the conclusion that the banishment was itself a curse, and if we note the evidence from Genesis 5 that the land Cain left behind sustained surprisingly lengthy lifespans. Given such a permanent separation between these two lands, and the compounded curse and punishment associated with Cain's new land, we may call the land of his banishment the "twice-cursed land," to distinguish it from the land he left behind, the "once-cursed land."

In addition, against the idea that Cain feared reprisals from his relatives, no mention is made of Adam and Eve's desire for retribution against Cain, and we have good reason to doubt that they would want to kill their own son, since he is their son. Likewise, we can doubt that any sibling or relative of Cain would feel compelled to bring vengeance, given God had already punished him. Further, the generality of כָּל־מֹצְאִי, "*all* who find me," in the phrase "all who find me will kill me"[13] speaks more as the reaction of a man with

---

11. These parallels are taken from Wenham, *Genesis 1–15*, 106.

12. Gen 4:15.

13. Gen 4:14.

imminent fear of strangers who outnumber him, rather than as a man afraid of unborn siblings tracking him down decades hence for retributive purposes. If he were heading to a place with no people at all, we would expect a lament to God about his loneliness, in the same way Adam had been alone, rather than an expression of his fear. Thus, it is likely that Genesis 4 implies that there were people from outside the garden in the land of Cain's banishment, and they were the ones he feared.

A further point can be made about Cain's wife. The text only records siblings of Cain after it mentions his wife, an ordering that inclines the reader to presume that he did not marry a sister, since at that point no sisters have been mentioned.[14] We can make a similar comment about the city that Cain built. The text records Cain building a city before mention of any of his siblings' births.[15] Again, this inclines the reader to assume that it was not a city full of Cain's siblings or cousins, since at that point no such siblings or cousins had been mentioned. The fact that Cain found a wife in the place of his banishment inclines the reader to conclude that the people Cain found in his new land were theological humans, if indeed there was ever any doubt on this question.

Moreover, we are told in Gen 4:25 that Seth was born "in the place of Abel." This inclines the reader to locate Seth and his progeny in the once-cursed land with Adam and Eve, where Abel had been, rather than in the twice-cursed land of Cain's banishment. Given that the offspring of Adam and Eve are separated from Cain, by some impassable barrier, we naturally conclude that the people who were with Cain had come from somewhere else, that is, from outside the garden.

In sum, when considered in isolation, given all this evidence, we may conclude that Genesis 4 is likely teaching that at the time of Cain's banishment, there were already full theological humans

14. Gen 4:17; cf. Gen 5:4. This point sits contrary to Jub 4:9, which recounts that Cain married his sister Awan. If this were so, it is plausible that Cain took his sister-wife into exile with him. This would not undermine the other arguments made in this section.

15. Gen 4:17.

in the place where Cain was banished. But perhaps other evidence overturns this conclusion. We turn then to consider Genesis 3:20.

PEOPLE FROM OUTSIDE THE GARDEN: THE OBJECTION FROM GENESIS 3:20

We have seen that Genesis 4, considered in isolation, is likely teaching that there were people from outside the garden, whom Cain met after his exile. However, there are other passages that seem to overturn that conclusion. In the remainder of the chapter, we will analyze two of these passages, Gen 3:20 and Acts 17:26.

Genesis 3:20 says, "Adam named his wife Eve, because she would become the mother of all the living." It is a passage that has produced considerable debate. In the seventeenth century, the French theologian Isaac La Peyrère wrote a work in Latin called *Prae Adamitae*,[16] "the pre-Adamites." In it, he argued that Adam was not the first human created by God, but merely the first of the Jewish race. He claimed that while the Jews were "formed by God in Adam," the Gentiles were created long before, "on the same day as other animate beings."[17] This pre-Adamite theory rightly attracted a number of critics, among them Reformed theologian Francis Turretin. However, while some of Turretin's criticisms were well made, one of them stemmed from Gen 3:20, and has implications for this discussion. He wrote that the pre-Adamite theory failed since Eve was "so named because she was the mother of all living (Gen. 3:20), which would be untrue if only the Jewish nation sprang from her."[18]

Turretin's point is a potential critique of any reading of Genesis that understands there to be people from outside the garden. For if Eve was אֵם כָּל־חָי, "the mother of all the living," in the sense that she was the biological ancestor of every human, then Cain

---

16. La Peyrère, *Prae-Adamitae*.
17. Quenstedt, *Theologia Didactico-Polemica*, 1:543.
18. Turretin, *Institutes of Elenctic Theology*, 1:457.

could not have met people descended from outside the garden, for no such people would exist.

To address this question, it is important to consider the events immediately preceding Adam's naming of Eve in Gen 3:20. Adam and Eve had just rebelled against God's command not to eat from the fruit of the tree of the knowledge of good and evil. In Gen 3:14–19, God pronounced his judgment on their rebellion, addressing first the serpent in 3:14–15, then the woman in 3:16, then finally the man in 3:17–19. At that point, immediately after Adam heard those curses, he named his wife חַוָּה, "Eve." We are told that he chose that name because "she would become the mother of all the living."[19]

There is debate about the meaning of the name חַוָּה, "Eve," with possibilities including "living,"[20] "Life-giver,"[21] and "Life."[22] Whatever the right translation, it is Wenham who asked the important question for our purposes, about the placement of Adam's declaration within the narrative:

> What prompted the man to call his wife "Life" especially at this juncture in the story? It comes immediately after the curses announcing man's mortality (v 19), the pains of childbirth (v 16), and the struggle of the woman's seed with the snake (v 15). Any of these curses could furnish the cue for the naming of the woman "Eve."[23]

Of these three options, only the struggle of the woman's seed with the snake represents a *new way* in which Eve would *give life*. The announcement of man's mortality is not an announcement of life, but an announcement of death. The idea of pain in childbirth is not a *new* announcement of life. For already in Gen 1:28, before the curse, humanity had been told, "be fruitful and increase in number," implying an expectation of childbirth for Eve. So, the

---

19. Gen 3:20.
20. See the footnote to Gen 3:20 in the NIV.
21. Layton, "Origin of Eve," 22–32.
22. Wenham, *Genesis 1–15*, 84.
23. Wenham, *Genesis 1–15*, 84.

only thing new in the announcement of pain in childbirth is the pain. Thus, the only element in these words that is both new and also points to Eve giving life is this: the promised battle between the woman's offspring and the snake.

The announcement of Gen 3:15 to the snake, that the offspring of the woman "will crush your head" has long been understood as the first statement in the Bible of the Christian gospel. This statement has been called the "protoevangelium," the "first gospel," by commentators,[24] since it represents the first promise that the ancient snake, Satan, would be destroyed, together with his works, and that he would be destroyed by a man descended from Eve. John Calvin expressed it this way: "that promise to crush Satan's head [Gen 3:15] pertains to Christ and all his members in common."[25]

So, it is possible to understand Eve to be the mother of all the living *in redemptive fashion*. That is, Eve is the mother of all who will live eternally, through the victory of Christ over Satan, since Christ is her offspring. This is an alternative to understanding that Eve is the mother of all the living *in biological fashion*, in which view she is the physical ancestor of every human.

This is not an original reading of the passage. Michael Lefebvre has argued,

> Examination of the text reveals that the designation "mother of all living" is not a reproductive notation: it is a soteriological statement. Genesis 3:15 . . . divides the human race into two categories: the seed of the woman and the seed of the serpent. Both "seeds" are groups of humanity. Adam called his wife "Eve". . . to identify her as "the mother of all living" with respect to the "seed" to arise from her in contrast with the human "seed" associated with the serpent . . . She is the mother of all who have the hope of life, not the mother of all humans.[26]

Which is more likely in the context? The fact that Adam's statement comes immediately after the protoevangelium lends

24. See for example Hamilton, *Handbook on the Pentateuch*, 46.

25. Calvin, *Institutes*, 1.14.18.

26. Lefebvre, "Adam Reigns," 52.

weight to the redemptive understanding. That is, the location of Adam's statement within the narrative suggests that Adam has responded to God's promise of redemption. He has responded by believing that eternal life will come through the woman's offspring, and so he has named Eve accordingly. This would suggest, incidentally, that in Gen 3:20 we see Adam not only understanding but expressing a confidence in God's promise of redemption.

On the other hand, in favor of taking Gen 3:20 in the traditional manner, in biological fashion, is that it is the easier reading to arrive at. There are a series of mental leaps required to move from the promise that Eve's offspring would crush the snake's head to a conclusion that Eve is therefore the mother of those living eternally because they will be redeemed through Christ's defeat of Satan.

Nevertheless, on balance, we may conclude that the redemptive understanding of Gen 3:20 is at least plausible. It retains the advantage, over the traditional understanding, of explaining why Adam speaks *at this point* as he does. So, this understanding of Gen 3:20 is not just attractive because it provides a reading consistent with there being people from outside the garden. It has further appeal and plausibility because it solves a genuine question independently posed by commentators. Namely, it answers why Adam named his wife "Life-giver" *in response to the curse.*

PEOPLE FROM OUTSIDE THE GARDEN: THE OBJECTION FROM ACTS 17:26

Acts 17:26 is another passage used by many to reject the theory that there were people from outside the garden. The context is that the apostle Paul was giving a speech in the city of Athens. In describing God's activity, Paul said, according to the NIV translation, "From one man he made all the nations, that they should inhabit the whole earth; and he marked out their appointed times in history and the boundaries of their lands." The key phrase, ἐξ ἑνός, is translated above as "from one man," but it is literally just saying, "from one," without specifying the referent, so that it could mean "from one man," or "from one nation," or "from one entity:" *From one, God made all the nations.*

In a debate about this verse in the context of origins, John Walton and Guy Waters disagreed over the referent of this phrase "from one." They agreed that a man is being referenced, but while Waters took the traditional view that the man is Adam, Walton argued that the one man is Noah. Walton wrote,

> If Paul were referring to Adam, we would expect him to use other vocabulary rather than "nations" to refer to all people . . . In fact, however, here the word choice is key because the Old Testament does talk about one man through whom the nations came—and that is Noah through his three sons . . . Paul's statement could easily be seen as a paraphrase of what is stated in Genesis 10.[27]

Waters countered by observing that the one man, Adam, is the "natural and expected counterpoint to the one man, Christ Jesus,"[28] and by noting that the phrase "on all the face of the earth" in Acts 17:26 echoes the teaching of Gen 1:28–29. So, he favors the one man being Adam, not Noah, because of the counterpoint to Christ that Adam represents, and because it was Adam who was being addressed in Gen 1:28–29, not Noah.

In weighing this debate, a number of further observations increase the plausibility of Walton's proposal that the spread of nations account of Genesis 10 is in view, rather than the fulfilling of the creation mandate, "be fruitful and increase in number," from Gen 1:28–29.

Firstly, the assertion that God "marked out their appointed times in history and the boundaries of their lands" points to Paul's thought pattern canvassing the movement of nations over time, rather than the creation mandate via biological expansion. This is because nations are defined particularly by their times in history, and the boundaries of their lands, whereas such considerations are not central to the fulfillment of the creation mandate to "be fruitful and increase in number."

27. Walton, "Archetypal Creation," 105.
28. Waters, "Incompatible with New Testament," 884–85.

Secondly, within the framework of Luke/Acts, an important theme is that the gospel must be preached and received among all *nations*.[29] Here too in Acts 17:26–27 we may understand that part of God's reason for establishing nations is so that the blessing of the gospel might come to nations *as nations*. So, we can read verse 27 as follows: "God did this," that is, he oversaw the spread of nations, "so that they," that is, nations, "would seek him and perhaps reach out for him and find him." So, we can plausibly say that the reason Paul is talking about *nations* is to underline his message that members of different *nations*, present at his speech, may now accept this blessing, as God has ordained for them to do. But this relies on Paul's thrust in Acts 17:26–27 being about the role of *nations* in God's economy, rather than about the success of the original creation mandate.

But if Paul is speaking about a socio-political spread of nationhood from one source in Noah's time, and not about the biological spread of humanity from Adam's time, then Acts 17:26 does not provide difficulty for this book's timeline, since it does not undermine the possibility that some of humanity might be derived biologically from outside the garden.

A third consideration regarding Acts 17:26 is text-critical in nature and explains why the church for so long held this verse to be talking about *biological* descent from Adam. The Western text of the Greek New Testament, together with other ancient Greek witnesses such as Irenaeus, Chrysostom, and Theodoret,[30] include the word αἵματος, "blood," in Acts 17:26. So, the KJV, reflecting this witness, says that God has made "from one *blood*, all nations of men." But the Greek word αἵματος, "blood," is not present in the earliest and most reliable New Testament witnesses, such as Sinaiticus and Vaticanus. As a result, modern English translations omit the word "blood."

---

29. Luke 2:32; 24:47; Acts 2:5; 9:15; 13:47; 28:28.
30. Aland et al., *Greek New Testament*, 463.

Thus, a large part of the historic church, from as early as the second century[31] to as late as the twentieth century,[32] was unaware that the word "blood" was likely omitted from the original text of Acts 17:26. Thus, an essential element of this book's proposal did not appear tenable to a great proportion of the historic church. For if we say that God made all nations "of one blood," and we also say, with the majority historical understanding, that "nations" here simply means "people," then we are speaking of a physical, material connection between all humanity, since blood is physical and material. This leads to the conclusion that all humanity has descended biologically from Adam, so that there could not have been people from outside the garden, since such people would derive from outside the biology of Adam. Thus, the presence of the word "blood" in Acts 17:26, accepted for such a long period of the church's history, has influenced theologians away from concluding that there could have been people from outside the garden.

Fourthly and finally, note that when the word "blood" is omitted from Acts 17:26, this new understanding can be suggested: it is now plausible to say that Acts 17:26 and Genesis 10 teach about the origin and spread of this socio-political entity called ἔθνος, גּוֹי, "nation." So, these passages may teach that nationhood did not spread before the era of Shem, Ham, and Japheth, or even that there were no nations at all before their arrival. These chapters may teach that such "nations" spread out *through existing populations*, as God directed, from one source. So, the point of Acts 17:26 and Genesis 10 would not then consist in peoples spreading out *into empty space on earth*. But rather the point would be that this new socio-political entity called a "nation" spread out, *from one man Noah*, or perhaps, *from one initial nation*, through the vast swathe of humanity that was already there.

A potential objection to this reading should be noted before we conclude the chapter. This objection is that it wrongly privileges the colonial West over the rest of the world. For according to

---

31. Irenaeus lived in the second century AD.

32. The KJV remained very influential through the early stages of the twentieth century.

the understanding of Acts 17 and Genesis 10 just outlined, nations spread out like a wave through existing people groups, starting from after the flood, c. 2900 BC. The potential objection, then, would be that this book's understanding leaves no room for the commonplace language of "first nations" to describe the ancient peoples of America, Australia, and the like.

By contrast, this chapter's understanding of these passages implies that nations, understood in the biblical sense, did not exist in the "New World" among the ancient peoples in places like Australia and the Americas, until after the time contact was made with them by those from the "Old World." Even if significant contact was made between the descendants of Noah and the ancient residents of the "New World" before journeys such as Columbus' and Cook's,[33] it would not seem sufficient to plant an entire new sort of socio-political entity, that which the Bible calls a "nation."

Thus, the objection would be that this book's thesis privileges Western culture and Western structures over other culture and structures, implying some sort of Western superiority depicted in their unique possession of the socio-political "nation." Chapter 4 will argue against this objection, but for now it should be noted that this is not a historical, scientific, or biblical objection, but a values-based objection. The objection will be addressed in due course. But that is a different and much easier task than defending Genesis 10–11 as historical, according to the traditional understanding of those passages. The main burden of this book is to propose an understanding of the early parts of the Bible consistent with mainstream science and history, and that question has now been addressed, at least regarding Acts 17:26. To answer further values-based objections lies at the periphery of this book's main goals.

Whatever the precise thesis on how Acts 17:26 and Genesis 10 describe the spread of nationhood, the key point is that possibilities exist consistent with there being people from outside the garden. For there are plausible understandings of Acts 17:26 and

---

33. Swamidass proposes significant such contact was made in his modeling of the spread of Adam and Eve's offspring. See Swamidass, *Genealogical Adam*, 65–78.

Genesis 10 that do not take the meaning to be about the biological spread of all humanity from one man, Adam.

CONCLUSION

This chapter has argued that it is consistent with a high view of Scripture to say that there are people from outside garden. The argument limited itself to three sections of Scripture, Genesis 4, Gen 3:20, and Acts 17:26, each within their own contexts.

We saw that, considered in isolation, Genesis 4 is likely teaching that at the time of Cain's banishment there were already full theological humans in the place where Cain was banished. We saw this in Cain's fear of being killed there, rather than fearing loneliness. We saw it in the unlikelihood of Cain's relatives entering his place of punishment to gain a vengeance God had already taken on him. We saw it in Cain's taking a wife there and in his building a city there. We saw it in the order the story was told, with no siblings mentioned until after Cain's banishment, and in the permanence of Cain's banishment, his permanent mark suggesting a permanent barrier between his old and new location. We labeled the land of Cain's banishment the "twice-cursed land" in distinction from the land he left behind, the "once-cursed land." These labels were grounded in the fact that the curse on Cain's farming compounded upon the curse on Adam, and are used as headings in our timeline.

Regarding Gen 3:20, we considered a reading of the passage that understood Eve to be "mother of all the living" in redemptive rather than biological fashion. We saw that despite this being a minority reading of the text, and despite it requiring a series of mental leaps, it holds the advantage of explaining why Adam called his wife "Life-giver" at the point in the story that he did, *immediately after the curse:* it was because she was to be the ancestor of the great Life-giver, Christ. So, we saw that this reading is not only consistent with there being people from outside the garden, but has plausibility independent of such a question. That is because it solves a genuine question independently posed by commentators about why Adam chose the moment he did to name his wife "Life-giver."

In considering Acts 17:26, we saw that the passage is plausibly talking about the spread of nations from the time of Noah, rather than the spread of biological humanity from the time of Adam. We saw this through observing the parallels between Acts 17:26 and Genesis 10, through noting Paul's emphasis on the times of the nations, on the boundaries of their lands, and on the theme within Luke-Acts of the gospel going to all nations. We also saw this through noting that it is only recently that the church has widely understood the passage not to mention the word "blood," as in the KJV, "hath made of one blood all nations of men."

However, those texts of Genesis 4, Gen 3:20, and Acts 17:26, as important as they are to the discussion, do not exhaust relevant scriptural material on the question of people from outside the garden. The next chapter will outline two theological objections to the notion of theistic evolution, outlined in a recent book by that name, *Theistic Evolution*. It will argue that these objections can be refuted plausibly, within the evolutionary framework endorsed by this book.

Chapter 3

Theological Objections to Theistic Evolution

INTRODUCTION

THE OPENING CHAPTER OF this book presented the strongest case known to this author that the chronology of the early parts of the Bible cannot be squared with what we know from science and history. That case was presented, not as the viewpoint of this book, but in order to make the need for this book clear, and to highlight the scale of the challenge. Such an opening demands a response to the assertion that the Bible does not hold up to scientific scrutiny. The case centered on the contention that the stated "begetting ages" of Genesis 5 and 11 can be added to make a timeline. But when such a timeline is calculated, multiple problems present themselves.

Chapter 1 proposed a timeline to account for these problems. A key innovative aspect of that timeline is its proposal that the world described in the early chapters of Genesis, the pre-flood world, was a physically separate world from that of our own. This possibility was defended especially by a study of 2 Pet 3:5–7, and a focus on its distinction between "the world of that time" and "the present heavens and earth." Chapter 2 addressed a notion entailed by the timeline, defending the possibility that there were humans whose biological source lay outside the garden of Eden.

This chapter will consider objections from Scripture to the notion of theistic evolution. Since a certain form of theistic evolution is embraced by this book's timeline, it is necessary to address critiques of theistic evolution. This will be done partly through interaction with Wayne Grudem, who has laid out twelve objections to theistic evolution within the edited volume *Theistic Evolution: A Scientific, Philosophical, and Theological Critique*.[1] As we consider two of Grudem's objections in detail, it will be argued that this book's timeline can be believed while also embracing a high view of Scripture. It will also be contended that this book's timeline and assumption set provide resources that can contribute to the mainstream scientific discussion on human origins.

DEFINING THEISTIC EVOLUTION

Before considering Grudem's objections to theistic evolution, it is worth considering the definition of the term "theistic evolution." Grudem defined it as follows: "God created matter and after that did not guide or intervene or act directly to cause any empirically detectable change in the natural behaviour of matter until all living things had evolved by purely natural processes."[2] While, as Grudem pointed out, there are authors who embrace theistic evolution defined in this way, his definition is too restrictive, scripturally speaking and otherwise. For Scripture speaks in various places of God intervening in our world, after his creation of matter, and there is no reason to insist he did not do so at certain stages of the evolutionary process. More than that, in our introduction we made the assertion that we do not consider a theory that involves God's miraculous direct intervention to be, for that reason alone, a theory outside of mainstream science. So, Grudem's definition is

1. Grudem, "Theistic Evolution," 784–85.
2. Grudem, "Theistic Evolution," 784.

not one that responds to the best case of his interlocutors. Others have shared this complaint.[3]

But rather than attempting our own full-fledged alternative definition of theistic evolution, it is enough to draw some lines within which this book's understanding of theistic evolution sits. The first point is that we embrace *to a significant degree* the key notions of the common descent of species and natural selection. The phrase "*to a significant degree*" is used because the timeline presented by this book modifies the common scientific account in this important way: We embrace the direct, special creation, by God, of many of the same species that evolved independently of such special creation. We further embrace the later blending of the evolved and the specially created, within their respective species. So, the understanding here is that biological humanity *both* evolved *and also* was created specially by God, and that these two separate sources of humanity later blended.

Such an understanding of theistic evolution might immediately raise questions for the reader as to why God needed to specially create a species that had already evolved, or cause the evolution of species that he was going to specially create. In brief, it is plausible that God used this dual mechanism of special creation and evolution because it suited his various purposes for humanity. So, we hypothesize that God created a suitable place for Adam and Eve in Eden, with its perfectly, specially created beings, for them to enjoy in their own perfection. He also created a suitable place for Cain to be sent after killing Abel, with all the horrors associated with evolution, "red in tooth and claw." That was to be a suitable place of banishment for the first murderer, and in the end, a suitable

---

3. Deborah Haarsma is a contributor to the edited book *Four Views on Creation, Evolution, and Design*. She wrote a review of the edited volume in which Grudem's chapter appeared, *Theistic Evolution: A Scientific, Philosophical, and Theological Critique*. In her review, she first stated that the "mirror" of the work *Theistic Evolution* was "aimed nearly directly" at those from Biologos, on whose site she posted the review, and she cited from *Theistic Evolution* to show as much. She went on to say of Grudem's definition that "No one at Biologos would describe God's action that way!" before showing how this important error undermined the book's arguments. See Haarsma, "Flawed Mirror," para. 7.

place for all humans who have fallen from our state of perfection. In this way, a dual mechanism of special creation and evolution can be seen as fitting to God's purposes for Adam, Eve, Cain, and the whole of humanity, according to our deeds and our nature.

The plausibility of this hypothesis regarding a two-stream creation of humanity, specially created and evolved, can be further seen by comparing it with the very similar proposal made in Swamidass's book *The Genealogical Adam and Eve*. Swamidass put his thesis this way:

> Entirely consistent with the genetic and archeological evidence, it is possible that Adam was created out of dust, and Eve out of his rib, less than ten thousand years ago. Leaving the garden, their offspring would have blended with those outside it, biologically identical neighbors from the surrounding area. In a few thousand years, they would become genealogical ancestors of everyone.[4]

Unlike Swamidass's contention, it is not advocated here that the evolved biological humans were "from the surrounding area" of Eden, at least not in such a way that they could travel back to the cherubim and flaming sword that guarded the way to the tree of life.[5] This is because this book's timeline locates the evolved humans in our own twice-cursed world. They were always in a place physically separate from the ancient once-cursed world, that is, physically separate from Eden and its surrounds. Likewise, the claim here is not that Adam and Eve would become genealogical ancestors of everyone within a few thousand years, though neither is that ruled out. But the contention is, leaning on Swamidass's contentions in *The Genealogical Adam and Eve*, that theistic human evolution, *even when combined with a thesis of special human creation*, may be credibly seen as a thesis that sits comfortably within the findings of mainstream science.

More than that, this book's understanding of theistic evolution is not limited merely to *human* evolution. Regarding the animal world, this book's view of evolution is such that it must

4. Swamidass, *Genealogical Adam*, 10.

5. Gen 3:24.

be able to accommodate the following: that many, though not all, animal species, including species of dove,[6] raven,[7] various crawling species,[8] flocks of livestock,[9] and more,[10] *both* evolved *and were also* created specially by God, with later blending of the specially created and the evolved, within their respective species. These then are the boundary markers of the theistic evolution that this book is defending as compatible with Scripture.

GRUDEM'S OBJECTIONS TO THEISTIC EVOLUTION

Despite the questionable nature of Grudem's definition of theistic evolution, his objections are important to consider. The edited volume *Theistic Evolution* is both substantial and recent, and it included numerous well-qualified authors contending against evolution from within a high view of Scripture. The best summary of the book's biblical objections to evolution are found in Grudem's twelve points. Ten of those are not relevant to this present work, since the form of theistic evolution they aimed to counter is so unlike that described here. However, two of Grudem's points very much need to be considered, as they strike at key elements of our presentation.

Adam and Eve Not the First Human Beings?

Grudem's first critique of theistic evolution was that, according to theistic evolution, "Adam and Eve were not the first human beings (and perhaps they never even existed)."[11] Grudem rightly argued from the larger structure of Genesis, especially the genealogies, that Genesis depicts Adam and Eve as real people.[12] To demonstrate the

6. Gen 8:7.
7. Gen 8:8.
8. Gen 8:17.
9. Gen 4:2.
10. Gen 8:17.
11. Grudem, "Theistic Evolution," 788–98.
12. Grudem, "Theistic Evolution," 794–96.

Bible's depiction of them as the *first* people, he focused on Matt 19:4–5, where Jesus mentions the first couple's creation *from the beginning*, as well as 1 Cor 15:45, where Paul explicitly calls Adam "the first man."[13]

We embraced this conclusion in our timeline in chapter 1, which depicted Adam and Eve as the first humans, by saying this: "*While there were 'biological humans' all over the world before Adam's sin, there were still no full humans until that event. There were 'biological humans' that looked like us, but they did not act like us fully, for they had not yet been given human souls—they were not 'theological humans' in the image of God before c. 5100 BC.*"

To be clear, our assumption here is that a "soul" is not part of our biology, and therefore not relevant to the term "species," which is a biological term. So, we are suggesting that for a short time around 5100 BC there was one biological species, two of whom, Adam and Eve, inside the garden, also had a human soul, while the others, who were outside the garden, did not. After around 5100 BC, there was still one biological species, but now every member of this biological species, Adam, Eve, and all the rest, had human souls. So, God gave all biological humans outside the garden a human soul at the same point in time, thus making them theological humans.

That is, our response to Grudem's critique hangs on the distinction introduced in chapter 1 between "mere biological humanity" and full "theological humanity," the latter having human souls, the former not. The phrasing above speaks of "human souls" as being provided to those who were at the time mere biological humans. This provision of souls was necessary, we hypothesize, before such beings could become theological humans, "in the image of God." Other language could potentially be used instead to express the same thought, such as that of God providing human "spirit" to beings that already had human bodies. What is necessary to assume is that beings could in prehistoric times look human and yet not be theologically human. What may be altered is the expression regarding that which they lacked, a "human soul," "human spirit,"

---

13. Grudem, "Theistic Evolution," 798.

or some combination or alternative to these phrases.[14] In this way, we can agree with Grudem that Adam and Eve were the first human beings, by which we understand the statement to mean they were the first theological humans, with both body and soul, even if there were beings before them who possessed mere biological humanity.

Not All Descended from Adam and Eve?

Grudem provided a second critique of theistic evolution, entitled "Not All Human Beings Have Descended from Adam and Eve." He argued for the physical descent of the entire human race from Adam on the basis that it "explains how the guilt of Adam's sin could be justly imputed to all his descendants, and it also provides the mechanism by which a sinful nature (or disposition toward sin) has been transmitted from generation to generation through-out the entire human race."[15]

This particular critique of theistic evolution underlines the reason that our timeline needed to hypothesize a great miracle of God across the globe at the time of Adam's sin: the miracle we hypothesize is that God used the soul of fallen Adam[16] as a model or source to provide what was lacking in the humanity of all *Homo sapiens* then alive on the planet.

If we assume that this occurred, we can avoid Grudem's critique. We can then say that even though not all humans are biologically descended from Adam, they have all sourced their humanity from Adam in an essential way. We can therefore say that all humans have inherited from Adam not only Adam's human dignity and worth in the image of God, but also the fallen aspects of his soul, making us all, like Adam, inclined to evil and worthy of death.

14. This is bound up with the discussion of the bipartite or tripartite nature of humanity. For commentary, with historic notes, see Berkhof, *Systematic Theology*, 191–92.

15. Grudem, "Theistic Evolution," 811.

16. Eve may have also been used as a model or source in similar fashion, but if so, only in such a way that we still can rightly say, "in Adam, all die."

Others may be able to suggest alternative routes to secure this result, consistent with this book's timeline. But without any such alternative being obvious to this writer, it seems necessary, in proposing this book's timeline, to assume the following: that some *non-material* element of Adam's humanity was used by God as a model or source for turning mere biological humans into full theological humans, at a single point in time, around 5100 BC. Put another way, evolved *Homo sapiens* needed a human "spark," a non-biological soul, before they could be fully human. God chose to provide this soul to a host of biological humans by first creating it in one man, Adam, and then relaying it from Adam to all the others.[17]

We further assume that God used Adam's *fallen* humanity as this model or source, that is, his humanity *after he sinned.* For this is how we may surmise that not just any humanity, but *fallen humanity bearing Adam's guilt,* came to inhabit our whole earth at that time. In this way, Adam's sinful nature was transmitted to the whole human race. This occurred first through the evolution and expansion of material, tangible, biological humanity across the globe, then by the miraculous bestowal of non-material, intangible, human souls to each such human, and finally through biological descent down to the present day. This not only secures the scriptural truth that Adam's sin was justly passed on to his descendants. It also secures the truth that the death that Adam justly deserved was also deserved by those whose fallen humanity was modeled on his. Thus, we can say, with the apostle Paul, that "in Adam all die."[18]

This proposal is not original. Derek Kidner proposed something very similar when he wrote,

> it is at least conceivable that after the special creation of Eve . . . God may have now conferred His image on Adam's collaterals, to bring them into the same realm of being. Adam's "federal" headship of humanity extended,

17. It is possible that God modeled or sourced the male souls from fallen Adam's soul, and modeled or sourced the female souls from fallen Eve's soul. If so, this was done in such a way that we may still say, "in Adam all die."

18. 1 Cor 15:22.

if that was the case, outwards to his contemporaries as well as onwards to his offspring, and his disobedience disinherited both alike.[19]

A KEY OBJECTION: ARCHAEOLOGICAL EVIDENCE FOR HUMAN ACTIVITY BEFORE 5100 BC?

This approach, with its date for the first human as late as 5100 BC, stands in contradiction to many mainstream writers in human evolution, as well as with Christian apologist William Lane Craig in his *In Quest of the Historical Adam.*

For his part, Craig's approach was to accept four "widely recognized conditions . . . sufficient for modern human behaviour . . . abstract thinking, planning depth, behavioural, economic, and technological innovativeness, and symbolic behaviour."[20] Having surveyed an extensive list of "archaeological signatures" of such modern behavior, he concluded as follows:

> The evidence of palaeoneurology concerning brain size and development inclines us to regard such ancient species as *Homo heidelbergensis and Homo neanderthalensis* as, like us, human. The manifold evidence of archaeology discloses archaeological signatures associated with the sufficient conditions for human cognitive capacity, especially art and language indicative of symbolic behaviour, that together provide a powerful cumulative case for the humanity of these same ancient species. Since these modern cognitive capacities did not in all probability evolve independently among ancient species of *Homo*, they are best regarded as inherited from a common ancestor, who is typically identified as *Homo heidelbergensis*, a large-brained, cosmopolitan species that may have originated anywhere in Eurasia or Africa prior to 750 kya . . . Adam and Eve may therefore be plausibly identified as members of *Homo heidelbergensis.*[21]

19. Kidner, *Genesis*, 29.
20. Craig, *Historical Adam*, 280–81.
21. Craig, *Historical Adam*, 358–59.

Craig's date for the first theological humans of 750,000 years ago is very early even by the standards of mainstream writers in evolutionary science. To see this, contrast his conclusion with the following two writers: Firstly, Yuval Harari, a professor of history and a populist writer, described a "cognitive revolution" in our ancient ancestors dating from around 70,000 years ago. He wrote,

> The period from about 70,000 years ago to about 30,000 years ago witnessed the invention of boats, oil lamps, bows and arrows and needles . . . The first objects that can reliably be called art date from this era . . . , as does the first clear evidence for religion, commerce and social stratification. Most researchers believe that these unprecedented accomplishments were the product of a revolution in Sapiens' cognitive abilities. They maintain that the people who drove the Neanderthals to extinction, settled Australia, and carved the Stadel lion-man were as intelligent, creative and sensitive as we are. If we were to come across the artists of the Stadel Cave, we could learn their language, and they ours. We'd be able to explain to them everything we know . . . and they could tell us how their people view the world.[22]

This was Harari's way of saying, in theological terms, they were full theological humans by c. 70000–30000 BC, though Harari himself would likely not use that term.

Moving to the center of respected scholarship on human evolution, Louise Humphries and Chris Stringer, researchers in human origins at the National History Museum, London, wrote this way regarding humanity's emergence:

> Humans used to be defined as "Man the Toolmaker," and the appearance of stone tools . . . was viewed as fundamental evidence for the emergence of humanity and our genus *Homo* . . . However, we now know that birds like crows . . . can make and use simple tools . . . Complex language has also been proposed as a defining feature of humans . . . How and when our ancestors progressed from ape-like language capabilities to those of humans

22. Harari, *Sapiens*, 23.

today is very difficult to read from the archaeological record. It was surely there in the hunter-gatherers who produced sophisticated cave art in Europe 35,000 years ago . . . A large brain in relation to body size is another human characteristic . . . However, the old view that there was a "cerebral Rubicon" that clearly separated all humans from all apes . . . has been repeatedly undermined by discoveries of small-brained fossil specimens that display many other human traits.[23]

What stands out for our purposes is the confidence that "complex language," said to be a "defining feature of humans," was "surely there . . . 35,000 years ago." Even though Humphries and Stringer were more measured than Craig or Harari in their claims about the emergence of humans, they still end up with a claim that around 35,000 years ago is the latest possible date for human emergence. The implication Humphries and Stringer drew is that those who produced sophisticated cave art must have had complex language, and therefore must have been fully human, as we are, no later than c. 35,000 years ago. The challenge for this book's timeline should be clear: if even the most measured writers claim clear evidence of full-fledged humanity existing well before 5100 BC, how can this book's timeline be maintained while claiming there were no theological humans before that time, and seeking to sit within mainstream science?

The first key point to make is to emphasize that the timing of full humanity's first appearance is at least as much a theological question as an archaeological one. Craig, Harari, Humphries, and Stringer have all made assumptions about what activities must be *necessarily* human, as well as assumptions about how such activities can be identified archaeologically. Craig himself, despite his high view of Scripture, has taken his assumptions in this area from secular anthropologists, rather than from the Bible. But the Bible does not share the assumption set of such anthropologists, nor of evolutionary biologists, regarding the nature of humanity.

---

23. Humphrey and Stringer, *Our Human Story*, 83–84.

The Scriptures in fact provide little detail from which we might extrapolate conclusions on the level of abstract thinking, planning depth, innovativeness, or symbolic behavior that the most advanced prehumans might have attained. It certainly does not address that question explicitly. More than that, we have not seen such creatures' behavior, since they were gone before we could observe them. So, these writers have been far more confident in their claims than the available data allows, certainly from a biblical point of view. Contrary to their overconfidence, the only archaeological evidence we would confidently accept for *necessarily* fully human behavior is that of written language, which does not appear in the record until after 4000 BC.

More than that, according to all these authors, there was a time when full humans coexisted with and bred with those who were not human, that is, to use the language of this book, there was a time when theological humans bred with those who were mere biological humans. This yields a disturbing picture, where God allowed confusion about whether beings that looked human should be treated with dignity as humans in his image or as lesser beings that may rightly be hunted or stolen from by those in need. It is a clear weakness in these reconstructions to posit such historic confusion. It is avoided by our assumption that God miraculously worked across our globe to bring all the mere biological humans of the time into full humanity in one instant.

Further, Craig's conclusion, with such an early date for Adam and Eve, is open to another critique: it is an open question whether members of *Homo heidelbergensis*, from as long ago as 750,000 years, could breed with modern *Homo sapiens* and produce fertile offspring.[24] So, Craig's conclusion may prove to be false on account of *Homo heidelbergensis* not possessing a truly human body.

But even without reference to Scripture or God, there is an important way to critique Humphries and Stringer's approach to the subject, according to their own assumption set. They themselves admit that language capabilities are very difficult to read

---

24. See the chart and commentary in Humphrey and Stringer, *Our Human Story*, 146–47.

from the archaeological record. Complex art *might*, of necessity, require language as complex as ours to produce. But this is not necessarily so. There is the real possibility that just as it was previously falsely assumed that animals cannot make tools, and cannot have a brain size equivalent to ours, so we might now falsely assume that the most advanced prehumans could not produce complex art.

We can come at that question from another direction, through considering the achievements of *Homo neanderthalensis*, for insight into what the most advanced prehumans could achieve. They are, generally speaking, not considered to be a form of human like us, notwithstanding Craig's arguments above. Certainly Humphries and Stringer did not consider Neanderthals to be fully human in *Our Human Story*. Yet they described their achievements this way:

> the Neanderthals probably also mounted stone points on wooden handles . . . to make short stabbing spears . . . there are some examples of geometric patterns made by Neanderthals on bones and stones . . . Despite claims to the contrary, it seems very likely that the Neanderthals buried their dead in caves where they had been living. Some burials suggest . . . possible ritualistic behaviour.[25]

The burial of the dead and ritualistic behavior could be described as "religious" behavior. And yet here Humphries and Stringer concede it may have been Neanderthal behavior. Geometric patterns move into the realm of art, and they are ascribed to Neanderthals. Thus, it should be seen as plausible that still further abilities would be possible in our theorized ancient group of *Homo sapiens who had not been endowed with human souls*. The point is that there is nothing in the Scriptures or in basic logic that would force us to rule that complex art, or even the ability to pronounce and understand some words, must be the sole domain of theological humans.

Is this to say that there are *no* traits or abilities that we would consider the sole domain of theological humans? No, it is not, since we can say, for example, that marriage is a state of being unique to theological humans, for the Bible presents Adam and

---

25. Humphrey and Stringer, *Our Human Story*, 90–91.

Eve as covenanting the first human marriage.[26] But marriage cannot be detected with certainty archaeologically without the presence of writing, describing a marriage. The big point, then, is that it remains plausible that the achievements of our biological ancestors, those who lived before 5100 BC, could be considered the achievements of mere biological humans, rather than necessarily achievements of full humans, those in God's image.

KEMP'S ALTERNATIVE WAY FORWARD

An entirely different way of tackling this problem was foreshadowed in chapter 1 and is worth addressing briefly. It was implied in Kemp's notion of the human "philosophical species." Recall that he defined the "philosophical species" as "the rational animal, i.e., a natural kind characterized by the capacity for conceptual thought, judgment, reasoning and free choice." We might hypothesize, then, that humanity from say c. 70000–5100 BC were examples of Kemp's "philosophical humans," while only after 5100 BC were the humans in existence full theological humans. This has an appeal that it would seem to spare us from disagreeing with Harari, Humphries, and Stringer above, if we take their joint claim to be that *Homo sapiens* from around 70000–30000 BC had come to possess the traits necessary to identify them as fully human.

Some might choose that path, and perhaps even still embrace the timeline of this book. However, that path has theoretical problems that seem best avoided. In particular, it is hard to see exactly why those hypothesized "philosophical humans" ought not to be considered fully human. Theoretically speaking, if such beings had full human capacity for conceptual thought, judgment, reasoning, and free choice, then by definition they would also have capacity for *fully human moral* thought, judgment, reasoning, and free choice. But humanity's capacity for *moral reasoning* seems hard to separate from key moral understandings that must be unique to humans. So, for example, humans come to understand much about themselves morally, both through moral reasoning, and

26. Gen 2:23–25; Mal 2:14; Matt 19:4–9.

through moral intuition.[27] They come to understand that they, as humans, possess a moral dignity and worth far greater than that of the animals, so that killing other humans is murder, but killing animals is not. They come to understand their obligations to love God and love human neighbors, to live in accordance with certain sexual norms defined with respect to the realities of human marriage covenants, and to live according to moral norms regarding possessions and the notion of stealing from other humans. But much of this human reasoning depends on an understanding of who the humans are, and that you are a human.

All this is to say that the nature of humanity is such that it can be doubted whether one can simply theorize the existence of a "philosophical human" that can reason as human but is not actually a theological human. Put another way, we expect that the differences between a human made fully in God's image and a mere biological human, not in God's image, would be quite clear. While our timeline denies that a full theological human ever interacted with a mere biological human, if they could be lined up and observed side by side, we are confident that the differences could be observed easily. So, a Kemp-style approach to human origins, proposing the existence of a "philosophical human" species, seems best rejected.

THEORETICAL RESOURCES THIS BOOK'S TIMELINE BRINGS TO ORIGINS SCIENCE

But in addition to defending our position against external critiques, and explaining possibilities we have rejected, it is also useful to show where the strengths of our proposal lie. There are theoretical resources gained by those who accept the timeline of this book. We will explore one of these before concluding this chapter.

The mainstream scientific position sees human evolution as a gradual process within a population of ancestral primates, so that it typically speaks of a continuum of changes rather than a

27. For a summary of how moral intuitions and moral reasoning interact with God justly holding us all to be without excuse for our failures, see Russell, *Seeing Good, Doing Evil*, 98–107.

singular first human. But such an approach, with its elimination of a sharp line between human and non-human, yields significant moral problems such as those caught up with interbreeding, sexual morality, murder, theft, and more.

It also means that there are genuine theoretical problems if writers want to propose that *Homo sapiens* were still developing traits and characteristics essential to their full humanity after c. 65000 BC in Europe or Africa. For in making such proposals, as some do, such writers may be implying that those traits or characteristics were developed *after* the outward migration of those who became the Australian indigenous peoples. Then the conclusion seems to be necessary that indigenous Australians may have missed out on a critical evolutionary leap, one that seems important to secure their full humanity, in theoretical terms.

This book's proposals offer a solution to avoid this conclusion. The timeline presented allows for a leap into full theological humanity to have occurred well after *Homo sapiens* had inhabited the whole planet, with no theoretical risk of anyone missing out. No one could have missed out because God himself superintended the endowment of full humanity globally. This approach means there is no need to place a theorized "cognitive revolution" prior to any particular migration of *Homo sapiens*. Thus, a wider range of positions on human uniqueness can be explored without inadvertently devaluing any population.

A further point is worth making in support of the Bible's timeline, before concluding. Harari was able to make this startling claim back in 2015: "The truth is that from about 2 million years ago until around 10,000 years ago, the world was home, at one and the same time, to several human species."[28] His figure of 10,000 years was based on a then-current consensus regarding the dating of *Homo floresiensis*. Since then, that dating has been revised backwards by around 40,000 years, making Harari's endpoint also 40,000 years too late.[29] The point is that the dating of the latest

---

28. Harari, *Sapiens*, 8.

29. Humphrey and Stringer, *Our Human Story*, 135.

non-*sapiens Homo* species has been in recent flux, and even a date as late as 10,000 years ago has been seen to be plausible.

Within this framework, consider this hypothetical question, asked from a God's-eye point of view: if God had decided to create just one species clearly marked out from the others, as those in his image, with commensurately distinct responsibilities, dignity, and value, then when would be the best time to bring this species into its full flower? That is, when would be the best time in now-known evolutionary history for God to have endowed the genus *Homo* with full theological humanity?

It seems clear that most fitting time would be *after Homo sapiens were established as the only species of Homo left on the planet*. For then there would be no doubt in any human's mind who the other humans are and who they are not. Then there would be no question of whether a half-caste Neanderthal-*sapiens* offspring is in fact fully human.

So, given that the most fitting time for this great leap is *after Homo sapiens were established as the only species of Homo left on the planet*, how does the Bible's timeline stack up? It stacks up remarkably well. For the Bible's timeline pinpoints c. 5100 BC as its date for Adam—a time clearly after the last non-*sapiens Homo* were extinct, on any timeline, including those drawn around 2015, when a very late *Homo floriensis* was widely accepted. The date of c. 5100 BC is fitting, then, because it clearly secures the result that at no time did any full theological human mate with a mere biologically human member of the *Homo* genus. It secures the result that no human had to ponder whether to treat other members of the *Homo* genus like someone in God's image or like a lesser being. And yet it is early enough that it clearly predates any archaeological evidence of writing, which is certain evidence of full human existence, and starts to appear in the fourth millennium BC.

CONCLUSION

What have we seen in this chapter? It has been argued that our timeline of human origins can plausibly be maintained in the face of objections that might come both from within mainstream science and from those with a high view of Scripture. The chapter has considered two objections from the scriptural side, namely that theistic evolution fails to be scriptural because it says Adam and Eve were not the first humans and also because it says we are not all descended from Adam and Eve. The defense to the first objection was to employ the distinction between mere biological humanity and full theological humanity, the latter but not the former having a human soul. This distinction enabled us to conclude that Adam and Eve may plausibly be considered to be the first humans, understood as theological humans, even while acknowledging that other biological *Homo sapiens* might have existed before them. The defense to the second objection was to agree that there have been humans in the image of God not descended from Adam and Eve, and to suggest a mechanism involving both special creation and evolution that enables us to say, with Paul, that "in Adam, all die." The proposed mechanism was that some *non-material* element of Adam's fallen humanity was used by God as a model or source for turning mere biological humans into full humans.

We have also provided a plausible answer as to how the date for the first full theological humans could significantly postdate complex cave art and evidence for other symbolic or ritualistic behavior. The answer was to note the significant achievements that may be attributable to Neanderthals, which are usually considered non-human. The answer was also to note that common assumptions about *uniquely human* behavior have been wrong in the past, because of underestimation of what animals can achieve. Modern contentions of a similar ilk could thus still be wrong for the same reasons, again underestimating the possibilities outside of theological humanity.

With this ground covered, it remains then in the next two chapters to consider how we might integrate the Genesis accounts of the flood and the Tower of Babel with the understandings of modern science. We begin with the flood.

Chapter 4

The Great Flood

INTRODUCTION

THE STORY OF THE flood offers great material for Sunday school, children's Bibles, and toys alike. It is a joyful thing to see children pull pairs of horses, elephants, chickens, and more from a toy boat as they learn about God. Of course, such is not the only use for the biblical story. The New Testament connects all sorts of important teaching to the flood, including the surprise of the coming of the Son of Man being like the surprise of the flood,[1] God's willingness to judge then and now,[2] the waters of the flood symbolising baptism,[3] Noah's rescue showing how God rescues the godly,[4] and Noah as a model of faith.[5]

But just as with Jesus' resurrection, where it is important to teach about both the historical fact and its meaning, so it is with

1. Matt 24:36–39.
2. 2 Pet 2:5.
3. 1 Pet 3:21.
4. 2 Pet 2:5–9.
5. Heb 11:7.

the flood. Whether we take the view that the narrative is history, protohistory, prehistory, theological history, ahistorical, or wholly unhistorical, the way we understand it impacts the conclusions we can draw from it, and our confidence in those conclusions.

This chapter will consider some alternate understandings of the meaning of the flood story and the historical reality behind it, focussing on those grounded in a high view of Scripture. In doing so, we will defend this book's timeline and assumption set as plausible—indeed at least as plausible as the main alternatives. Our hypothesis is that Genesis describes the flood destroying a world that was distinct from our own. That is, Genesis describes Cain as being banished from the world of his parents, from the world this book calls the "once-cursed world," into our own world, which this book calls the "twice-cursed world."[6] Our claim is that it is plausible that it was this once-cursed world destroyed by flood, and not our own twice-cursed world. Our claim also is that this is at least as plausible as the major alternatives grounded in a high view of Scripture.

THE TRADITIONAL VIEW: OUR WHOLE WORLD WAS FLOODED

One of the repeated elements of the Genesis flood account is its emphasis that the flood was to destroy all life. This element is worth reviewing in detail, to make clear why many have concluded from the biblical account that a total flood of our whole world is communicated. At the outset of the flood narrative, Gen 6:6–7 explains why God sent the flood:

> The Lord regretted that he had made human beings on the earth, and his heart was deeply troubled. So the Lord said, "I will wipe from the face of the earth the human race I have created—and with them the animals, the

---

6. The curses being referenced are, respectively, the curse on Adam and the curse on Cain, in particular the curse on the fruit of their labor in farming the ground. See Gen 3:17–19 and Gen 4:10–12.

birds and the creatures that move along the ground—for
I regret that I have made them."

According to normal assumptions about our world, if the human race, as well as all the animals, birds, and ground creatures were to be wiped from the earth by a flood, one would think such a flood would cover the whole of our globe, since animals and humans have long been found across the whole globe.

The universality of the destruction is underlined again in Genesis 7, where the reason for taking the animals on the ark is given, and again it is made clear that every animal is going to perish:

> Take with you seven pairs of every kind of clean animal . . . to keep their various kinds alive throughout the earth. Seven days from now I will send rain on the earth for forty days and forty nights, and I will wipe from the face of the earth every living creature I have made.[7]

Since we are told that the animals were placed on the ark in order to keep their various kinds alive, we easily conclude that no animals survive outside the ark. This is because if the ark is keeping the kinds alive, presumably they are not still alive outside the ark. This seems especially likely when we read that Gen 7:4 says that God will wipe from the face of the earth אֶת־כָּל־הַיְקוּם, "every living creature,"[8] he has made.

By the end of the story, after the flood has risen to its height, it is stated that God did not fail in his task to wipe out everything that breathes. This is restated three times in Gen 7:20–24:

> The waters rose and covered the mountains to a depth of more than fifteen cubits. כָּל־בָּשָׂר, *Every living thing* that moved on land perished—birds, livestock, wild animals, all the creatures that swarm over the earth, and all mankind. כֹּל, *everything* on dry land that had the breath of life in its nostrils died. אֶת־כָּל־הַיְקוּם, *every living thing* on the face of the earth was wiped out; people and animals and

---

7. Gen 7:2–4.

8. This Hebrew construction is referring to the non-human, non-plant creatures.

the creatures that move along the ground and the birds
were wiped from the earth.

So, it is reinforced three times with the word כֹּל, "everything,"
that everything perished.

Even after the fact of the flood, in Gen 9:11, this universal destruction is further reinforced, when God promises never to do it
again: "I establish my covenant with you: never again will כָל־בָּשָׂר,
all life, be destroyed by the waters of a flood; never again will there
be a flood to destroy the earth."

So, it is said that all life would be destroyed, that it was destroyed, and that it will never be destroyed again. One therefore
has good reason to conclude this is one of the most important
points Genesis makes about what happened at the flood. One can
see why many[9] over the years have concluded that the passage
teaches that our entire globe was flooded, including lands the first
author could not have named, such as Australia or North America.

Modern adherents of such a position have proposed an approach known as flood geology. Advocates of flood geology argue
that fossils, distributed globally as they are, are evidence of the
great biblical deluge across our globe, because the pressure from
the floodwaters produced the fossils. Prominent proponents include Henry Morris, John Whitcomb, Steven Austin, and Andrew
Snelling.[10] Such proposals sit sufficiently outside of mainstream
science that we will not spend much time in critique of them. It is
enough to say that there is good evidence to reject the notion that
fossils are evidence of a global flood in our world.[11] As we saw in
the opening chapter, a key critique of the global flood hypothesis
is well expressed by Richard Dawkins, and regards the distribution
of animals in our world:

9. Augustine was one example in this camp. He argued for the plausibility
of water being able to reach the heights of the high mountains. See Augustine
of Hippo, *Questions on Genesis*, ch. 7.

10. Some of the more prominent books advocating flood geology include
Morris and Whitcomb, *Genesis Flood*; Austin, *Grand Canyon*; Snelling, *Earth's
Catastrophic Past*.

11. See for example Moshier, "Worldwide Flood," 150–61.

think what the geographical distribution of animals should look like if they'd all dispersed from Noah's Ark. Shouldn't there be some sort of law of decreasing species diversity as we move away from an epicenter—perhaps Mount Ararat? I don't need to tell you that that is not what we see. Why did the entire order Edentata (all twenty species of armadillo, including the extinct giant armadillo, all six species of sloth, including extinct giant sloths, and all four species of anteater) troop off unerringly for South America, leaving not a rack behind, leaving no hide nor hair nor armour plate of settlers somewhere along the way? . . . Now there are thirty-seven species of lemur (plus some extinct ones). They range in size from the pygmy mouse lemur, smaller than a hamster, to a giant lemur, larger than a gorilla and resembling a bear, which went extinct quite recently. And they are all, every last one of them, in Madagascar. There are no lemurs anywhere else in the world, and there are no monkeys in Madagascar. How [did] this state of affairs come about? Did all thirty-seven and more species of lemur troop in a body down Noah's gangplank and hightail it . . . for Madagascar, leaving not a single straggler by the wayside, anywhere throughout the length and breadth of Africa?[12]

The point should be clear: the animals in our world do not look to be distributed around the globe as though they all came from the same boat five thousand years ago or less. That is evidenced not just by the fact that the marsupials are only found in Australia, New Guinea, neighboring islands, and parts of the Americas, but also by the distribution of many other species, including extinct species. This makes the hypothesis that our whole globe was flooded and the animals replenished only from Noah's ark highly implausible. It is likewise highly implausible to impugn God's character by claiming that he made it look as though there was no global flood, even though there was, in order to test us, or for some other reason. It is hard to see why such a God could not rightly be described as deceitful.

12. Dawkins, *Greatest Show*, 268–69.

LONGMAN AND WALTON'S APPROACH

So, others take the view that what we have in Genesis 6–9 is a retelling of the popular flood myths of the time, the point being to focus not on the descriptions, but the *interpretations* of the existing myths. So, on this view, it is where Genesis *changes* the original story that we see the authoritative word of God, not in the story's descriptions of events. In a popular book *The Lost World of the Flood*, Tremper Longman and John Walton said "there is a real world . . . the Bible does not *describe* that world authoritatively . . . But, the Bible does *interpret* that world authoritatively."[13] They went on to say it is clear that some details of the flood story are exaggerated, and everyone knew that at the time as well as now.[14]

One problem with this approach is as follows: only when we know the original myth can we know what has been changed by Genesis and what has not. But we do not know precisely what the original myths were that the author of Genesis had in mind. So, on this view, we cannot work out with confidence what the inspired element is and what is just repeated myth, with no true history behind it. If we do not know the original myth, we cannot know what is the changed, inspired *interpretation* and what is the unchanged, mythological, non-inspired *description*. This is a problem for understanding the flood narrative, for knowing the history behind it, and for our doctrine of Scripture, since it is problematic to say we don't know which parts of the Bible are the inspired word of God and which aren't.

More than that, the Genesis story goes out of its way to date the events precisely, which is not what we would expect if the main point were the interpretation of a myth that does not care about historical dates. So, we are told in Gen 7:11, "In the six hundredth year of Noah's life, on the seventeenth day of the second month—on that day all the springs of the great deep burst forth." The phrase בַּיּוֹם הַזֶּה, "on that day," emphasizes the interest in the dating, as does the follow up in Gen 7:13, בְּעֶצֶם הַיּוֹם הַזֶּה, "on that

---

13. Longman III and Walton, *Lost World of the flood*, 11.

14. Longman III and Walton, 38.

very day," as does also the explicit connection to the life of Noah, whose timeframes are linked all the way back to Adam in Genesis 5. So, Genesis does care about the specific date of the flood event, and about the history. This is a problem for Longman and Walton's approach, since they have assumed that the key thing the early chapters of Genesis care about is not the historical descriptions, but the interpretations of prevailing myths.

Related to this is Longman and Walton's answer regarding whether the flood story has a real event behind it. While they affirmed that Genesis narrates a truly global flood, they suggested that the real-world referent behind the flood myth was a significant local flood. They mentioned two examples of the kind of flood they had in mind, but also insisted that they are "not saying that one of these events is definitely the historical source of the flood stories of the Bible and the ANE." Their best example came from the research of William Ryan and Walter Pitman, who concluded that a flood "burst through Bosporus in 5600 B.C. so violently [that it] cleaved Europe from Anatolia."

This would be more plausible if the Genesis author did not take such pains to locate the narrative in history. But as we have already seen, the Genesis author did take great pains to do so, and the timeline implied by its genealogies places the flood somewhere between 3300 and 2050 BC. Nevertheless, Longman and Walton were happy to propose an event and a date for the real-world flood that sits outside of these plausible ranges of dates. This closes the door to a large number of possible hypotheses regarding the connection between the Genesis story and history, and so makes their proposal less plausible.

OTHER APPROACHES

So, others point out that the word אֶרֶץ, "earth," can be translated "land" as well as "earth," and suggest that the text might simply be saying that a local *land* was completely flooded. In the notes to the *ESV Study Bible* on Gen 6:17, T. Desmond Alexander wrote,

> Since the geographical perspective of ancient people was more limited than that of contemporary readers, it is possible that the flood, while universal from their viewpoint, did not cover the entire globe . . . a huge regional flood may have been all that was necessary for God to destroy all human beings. The expression "all the earth" does not exclude such a possibility; later, "all the earth" came to Joseph to buy grain (41:57), in which "all the earth" clearly refers to the eastern Mediterranean seaboard.[15]

Yet the Genesis author knew about Mount Ararat, which Alexander suggested is 5,137 meters high,[16] implying that an implausible amount of water would be required to cover it. More than that, if the view is that Genesis communicates that a global flood occurred *that in fact did not occur*, we are left needing to employ a similar distinction to Longman and Walton's if we are to maintain a high view of Scripture. That is, we need to propose a distinction between the non-authoritative descriptions and the authoritative interpretations of the myth, or find some other way to hold that this part of Scripture is authoritative while it describes things that did not happen. We have already mentioned some of the problems with such an approach, as it pertains to the flood story.

If, on the other hand, we take the view that Genesis intends to communicate a *local* flood, a flood that was universal to those who experienced it, but in fact did not cover the whole globe, then the text itself appears incoherent. For it is hard to see how Noah's ark was needed to save all these species of animals and kinds of food, if many of them were going to survive outside the ark anyway. One stated purpose of having the animals on the ark, after all, was "to keep their various kinds alive on the earth."[17] So, the approach to the story suggested by Alexander either shares the problems of Longman and Walton or appears incoherent.

So, others say, it does not matter what actually happened. It is the meaning, not the fact, we should focus on. But with these

---

15. Alexander, "Genesis Study Notes," 62.
16. Alexander, "Genesis Study Notes," 62.
17. Gen 7:3.

historical narratives, to find the meaning, we need a view of what actually happened. So, for example, if we are trying to explain the meaning of God's statement that "I am surely going to destroy . . . all people . . . and the earth,"[18] we need to have a view both as to what God said he would do and whether he actually did it. If we are saying it does not matter what God did, we are also saying it does not matter what God said he would do, for surely God did what he said he would do. So, this viewpoint ends up conceding either that it does not matter what God did or said in this part of the Bible or simply that God has been unable to communicate clearly through much of the flood story.

"TWO WORLDS" BIBLICAL DATA IGNORED BY THESE APPROACHES

We have seen then that these approaches each have their own weaknesses. But there is also a potential weakness shared by them all. It stems from the fact that they all ignore the possibility that Genesis might be teaching the existence of two separate worlds, one destroyed by the flood and the other not. The stronger the evidence that this is taught by Genesis, the weaker these approaches will be when they overlook this evidence. In this section, we will therefore ask: in the flood account and its wider context, what evidence do we find for a distinction between two physically separate worlds, one destroyed by the flood and the other not? Five pieces of evidence are noteworthy.

The first piece of evidence comes from the flood account's teaching that not only were the animals to be wiped out, but also that the *earth was to be destroyed*. So, Gen 6:13 tells us, "I am surely going to destroy both them and the earth." Gen 9:11 says, "never again will there be a flood to destroy the earth." In both Gen 6:13 and 9:11, the Hebrew root used for "destroy" is שחת, a root whose semantic range includes to "ruin," "destroy," or "annihilate." It is plausible to conclude from the use of this word that the earth

---

18. Gen 6:13.

described at the start of the flood story is no more by the time of the end of the story. It was destroyed, such that it is not able to be inhabited again. The waters are said to have flooded the earth for 150 days.[19] Both modern and original readers can be expected to know that the vast majority, or indeed all, of trees and plants cannot come back to life after 150 days under deep water. So, both then and now, we can plausibly read the text as saying that the world of that time was destroyed, that is, rendered permanently uninhabitable. In chapter 1, we saw that Gen 7:11 describes the opening of the אֲרֻבֹּת, "doors," of the הַשָּׁמַיִם, "firmament," to flood the world, in a way that plausibly reads as a permanent destruction of the heavens, since the water above the firmament could only be released once. If this is accepted as the best reading of Gen 7:11, it fits best with the account depicting two physically separate worlds, one that was destroyed by the flood, and the other where the narrative continues after the flood.

Secondly, given an expectation that 150 days under deep water should destroy all land-based life, we are left to ponder what is intended by the account in chapter 8, when Noah sent out a dove. Gen 8:11 tells us, "When the dove returned to him in the evening, there in its beak was a freshly plucked olive leaf!" The exclamation mark translates the word הִנֵּה, "behold," from the Hebrew. This is surely pushing us to see that a miracle of some kind has occurred. But what is the miracle? It is less plausible to conclude that the miracle is that God made all our world's plant life survive 150 days underwater, and then made all the water disappear. It is more plausible to suggest that the miracle is that God brought Noah's ark from the once-cursed world that Cain was banished from into our twice-cursed world, that is, into our physically distinct world where the curse on Cain had compounded on the curse on Adam. That is, the length of time of the flood, and the relative probabilities surrounding the miracle behind Gen 8:11, bolster the plausibility that the text is teaching two physically distinct worlds.

This is true *even within a framework like Longman and Walton's*. That is, even if we think the authoritative section of text is

19. Gen 7:24.

only where Genesis interprets a preexisting myth, and not where it repeats the descriptions of that myth, we still first have to decide what Genesis is saying in its own terms. Only then can we decide, even on Longman and Walton's assumption set, whether Gen 8:11 is authoritative interpretation or non-authoritative description. Is Gen 8:11 saying there was a miracle of trees and plants miraculously surviving 150 days underwater, or is it saying Noah's ark has just been brought miraculously from a distinct physical world where Adam and Eve once lived? If the first readers knew that the mountains of Ararat were in the order of five thousand meters high, needing an implausible amount of water to cover, and if they also knew that trees and plants do not survive 150 days under water, it is reasonable to assume they would consider the second explanation to be at least as plausible as the first.

A third piece of biblical evidence pointing to two distinct physical worlds relates to the lifespans of the patriarchs before and after the flood. That is, the Genesis account depicts the lifespans of these patriarchs declining through the generations, but *only after the flood*. The lifespans of the patriarchs before the flood were typically around 900 years. There is no discernible systematic reduction in expected lifespan from the time of Adam with his 930 years, to Noah, with his 950 years.[20] It is only *after the flood*, and *immediately after the flood*, that these lifespans decline, according to Genesis. God explicitly says that he will reduce human lifespans to 120 years *immediately before the flood, as part of the introduction to the flood narrative*.[21] With Wenham, it is best to understand this to mean that this maximum lifespan "was only gradually implemented"[22] after the flood, the implementation taking many generations.

When the ages do decline, according to Genesis 11, they do so according to an approximate sigmoid curve, that is, quickly at first, then more slowly, arriving at a modern length of lifespan,

20. See the appendix for a table depicting the respective ages of the patriarchs.

21. Gen 6:3.

22. Wenham, *Genesis 1–15*, 142.

only after thirteen or more generations.[23] This suggests that Genesis is presenting two very different physical worlds: the pre-flood world, which supported very long lifespans, and the post-flood world, which does not. It suggests God chose to bring Noah and his family into this new world *in order to carry out his stated intention to reduce human lifespans.*

It also suggests two different lineages of humanity: The first was derived biologically from the pre-flood world, and associated with exceptionally long lifespans, which continued for a time when brought into our world. The second was derived biologically from our world and possessed "normal" lifespans. This would mean that for a time there were a small number of long-lifespan individuals who were brought by God into the midst of a large number of normal-lifespan individuals.

This conclusion is made more likely by the account of Jacob's meeting with Pharaoh in Gen 47:8–9: Pharaoh asked him, "How old are you?" And Jacob said to Pharaoh, "The years of my pilgrimage are a hundred and thirty. My years have been few and difficult, and they do not equal the years of the pilgrimage of my fathers." The fact that Jacob feels the need to explain to Pharaoh that his lifespan is both shorter and more difficult than his ancestors pushes us to conclude that Pharaoh has not experienced the same phenomena. If this were the experience of every person at that time, then we expect Pharaoh would be aware of the declining lifespan experience and would not need it explained to him. But the way Jacob answers the question leads the reader to think that Jacob and his family were special in this regard. It leads us to conclude, therefore, that Jacob was part of a small group of long-lifespan individuals descended from Noah, in the midst of a much larger group of normal-lifespan individuals who were not descended from Noah. And that is why this is a startling revelation from Jacob, remarkable enough to be the only recorded question and answer in Jacob and Pharaoh's exchange. The fact that Jacob declared his age within the narrative and declared his 130 years to

23. Joseph lived one hundred and ten years, the first of the patriarchs to die at an age we might consider plausible by modern standards.

be few also pushes us to conclude that Genesis wants us to take the chapter 5 and 11 age data at face value, a conclusion at odds with positions like that of Longman and Walton.[24] Alternative theories for the extended lifespans after the flood, such as a life-extending vapor canopy remaining for a time in the heavens,[25] fail to account for the newsworthy nature of Jacob's longevity.

This suggests the explanation that Noah's descendants had to deal with more difficult life conditions in our world, compared to the once-cursed world they left behind. It suggests that as Noah's offspring bred with those who had always been subject to twice-cursed-world lifespans, the expected lifespan of their offspring declined steadily toward ours. That is, the account of the lifespan decline can be explained better using a two-worlds hypothesis, compared with other accounts.

For those who reject a two-worlds reading of the text and treat the long lifespans of Genesis 5 and 11 as hyperbole or symbolism, other problems emerge in reading the Genesis account. For as the Genesis account moves beyond chapter 11 into material that Longman, Walton, and others accept as historical, they need to reckon with the ongoing long lifespans of men such as Abraham with his 175 years[26], Jacob with his 147 years,[27] and Moses with his 120 years.[28] They need to reckon with the fact that Abraham's wife Sarah still looked beautiful enough to be taken by Pharaoh for his harem, when she was at least 65 years old.[29] These very long lifespans are recorded despite sitting outside the purported proto-history section of Genesis 1–11. A two-worlds reading can happily

24. They reject the notion that the age data of Genesis 5 and 11 can be added to produce a timeline on the basis of a cursory mention of Green's work, the flaws in which were outlined in this book's introduction. See Longman III and Walton, *Lost World of the Flood*, 108.

25. For this theory, see Morris and Whitcomb, *Genesis Flood*, 399–405.

26. Gen 25:7.

27. Gen 47:28.

28. Deut 34:7

29. Gen 17:17 suggests that Sarah is ten years younger than Abraham. Gen 12:4 states that Abram was seventy-five when he left Haran, so Sarah can be no younger than sixty-five when Pharaoh takes her, having heard of her beauty.

embrace these dates. Yet they are unexplained by the likes of Long-man and Walton, who reject them historically, and in terms of the Genesis narrative do not explain why, if the protohistory ends at Genesis 11, the expansive lifespans continue so long afterwards. This points to the relative weakness of accounts that reject a two-worlds reading of the text.

A fourth piece of evidence centers on the water cycle de-scribed in the early parts of Genesis. There is a good case that Gen-esis presents the water cycle and rainbows of our world as different from that of pre-flood times. Genesis 2 tells us that "no shrub had yet appeared on the earth and no plant had yet sprung up, for the Lord God *had not sent rain* on the earth . . . but streams came up from the earth and watered the whole surface of the ground . . . A river watering the garden flowed from Eden."[30] The first time rain is mentioned in the narrative is with the flood itself, and in or-der for that to occur, we are told, "the floodgates of the heavens were opened. And rain fell on the earth for forty days and forty nights."[31] So, the later introduction of the rainbow, after the flood, may indicate that there was no rain at all in the pre-flood world, or alternatively that something in the makeup of rain and sun was so different after the flood, compared to before, that rainbows are possible in our world, whereas in the pre-flood world they were not. This significant change makes more plausible the conclusion that an entirely different physical world is being narrated pre- ver-sus post-flood.

Moreover, if the rainbow itself was already familiar to Noah and his family, then the verb נָתַתִּי, "I have set," in Gen 9:13 would not seem natural: "I have set my rainbow in the clouds." If the rain-bow had been a past feature of their world, we would expect God to simply say, "The rainbow that you have known now becomes the sign of this covenant." The addition of "I have set" makes it more likely that the rainbow is a new feature, now introduced be-cause of this new covenant.[32] Additionally, we can say that since

30. Gen 2:5–6, 10.
31. Gen 7:10–11.
32. This understanding has historically been defended, without being the

the covenant of Gen 9:12–17 is newly established, it is fitting that its sign should be new. But if the reader concludes that the rainbow is a new feature, they can reasonably conclude that it is a new feature because Genesis is narrating a new physical world that Noah has entered, post-flood.

A fifth way that Genesis suggests physical differences in the pre-flood world, compared to the post-flood world, is seen in the changed relationships between animals and humans expressed in Gen 9:2–3: "The fear and dread of you will fall on all the beasts of the earth, and on all the birds in the sky, on every creature that moves along the ground, and on all the fish in the sea; they are given into your hands. Everything that lives and moves about will be food for you. Just as I gave you the green plants, I now give you everything."

Commentators have pointed out the parallels between Gen 9:1–7 and the opening chapter of Genesis, including the repeat of the blessings on humanity from Gen 1:28–29, the modifications of the food laws, and reassertion of the sanctity of life.[33] What should be noticed for our purposes is that this implies both a permanence and a universality to God's statements in Gen 9:2–3, just as the statements in Genesis 1 were permanent and universal. The prefix in the word כְּיֶרֶק, rightly translated "just as" in the NIV in Gen 9:3, helps to underscore this connection: "*Just as* I gave you the green plants, I now give you everything."

We can ask which understanding of the narrative fits with this change most naturally, the traditional "one curse, one world" framework or our "two worlds, two curses" framework: if we assume, with the traditional viewpoint, that there was just one curse and one world, when would we expect a change where the fear of humanity falls on all the animals? It seems the answer should

---

majority view. So, Calvin wrote, "From these words certain eminent theologians have been induced to deny that there was any rainbow before the deluge: which is frivolous. For the words of Moses do not signify, that a bow was then formed, which did not previously exist; but that a mark was engraven upon it, which should give a sign of the divine favour towards man." Calvin, *Genesis*, 299.

33. Wenham, *Genesis 1–15*, 192.

be, immediately after the curse on Adam and Eve and the serpent, since it was that curse that uniquely had universal consequences for humans and animals, in that framework. Wenham, following commentators C. F. Keil and Willem Gispen, admitted as much when he said regarding the animals' fear, "this seems more likely to reflect the animosity between man and the animal world that followed the fall (3:15) than the animals' unpleasant experiences in the flood."[34] This is an admission that the traditional understanding does not fit the text well at this point, because it is not very plausible that localized bad experiences on the ark should produce universal enduring change in animal-human relations. Yet the text underscores that a permanent universal change is now occurring, after the flood, when Noah is informed, using the imperfect tense, rightly translated in future time, that fear and dread of him יִהְיֶה, "will fall." This future time implies that the animals did not have that same disposition of fear and dread in the past, in Noah's experience. It fits the text more plausibly, then, to suggest that the permanent universal change in view is a change in Noah's experience as he moves from the once-cursed world to the twice-cursed world, after the flood.

From a different angle, the permanent nature of the change in animal-human relations after the flood is so significant that it could be plausibly argued to be the most significant element in the story, since it is an enduring, permanent change affecting both human and animal, more than any other change that the flood produces. In this, we can see another weakness in Longman and Walton's approach: having abandoned the notion that the text describes what actually occurred, their conclusion that a historical local flood occurred at all is a subjective choice.

Why should a local flood be the key historical kernel in the story, when even less might have been required to produce some change in animal-human relations that could have given rise to this story? It seems just as plausible to argue that the historical kernel behind the story might have been, say, a change in the course of a significant river, which so disrupted and scared the animals

34. Wenham, *Genesis 1–15*, 192.

that there was a significant change in human-animal relations in the area, perhaps including new meat-eating tendencies among the people who lived there. We are not advocating for such a proposal, to be clear. But we mention it to point out that for Longman and Walton, nothing at all can be said with confidence about what actually occurred, as background to the flood narrative. Their approach is inherently subjective when considering the historical background of this part of the Bible, and this renders their account less plausible.

Drawing things together, the cumulative weight of all this data becomes weightier still when we observe the proportion of important elements of the flood story that have been surveyed. From the context of an Edenic world with no rain, to the nature of Cain's banishment, to the mechanism by which the flood came, to the depth of water and the duration of the flood, to the nature of animal-human relations before and after, to the rainbow, to the lifespans before and after the flood, it is hard to find an element of the flood story that does *not contribute* to the case that Genesis describes two distinct physical worlds, one destroyed by a flood and the other not. The more the cumulative weight of all this biblical data is acknowledged as pointing to a two-worlds reading of the story, the more we must also acknowledge weaknesses in the existing understandings of Genesis that reject it.

OUR ALTERNATIVE

Thus, we have seen many weaknesses in the existing major accounts. These are significant enough that those with a high view of Scripture should be looking for a better way forward. Let us then lay out our alternative proposal.

Our alternative proposal is to accept that the story of the flood in its context is read most naturally as describing two physically distinct worlds, one flooded and the other not. Our proposal is to accept the age data for the patriarchs at face value, to create a timeline using it, and to date the flood accordingly. Our timeline, as seen in chapter 1, proposes that in both the text of Genesis, and in reality, there were two physically separate worlds. It proposes that one of these worlds, the world of that time, was deluged and destroyed somewhere in the range 3300–2050 BC, with a best estimate of 2900 BC. Our proposal is that we call our world the "twice-cursed world," and understand that it was never destroyed by a flood, as opposed to the world that was, the world that we call the "once-cursed world."

From a different angle, our proposal is that Noah spent 600 years in the once-cursed world. Then, with his family members and many kinds of animals and food, he entered the ark he had built. Then God destroyed that world with the flood. Then in a miraculous fashion God brought the ark and its contents to our world. Then Noah and his family exited the ark. Finally, Noah spent a further 350 years in our twice-cursed world.

Within this framework, it is not at all clear that any of the descriptions of Genesis 6–9 must be exaggerated hyperbole, as claimed by Longman and Walton.[35] As such, our understanding has the strength that we do not need to make their distinction between the authoritative *interpretations* of the facts and the non-authoritative *descriptions* of the facts. We may simply read what is written as though it occurred, according to the two-worlds framework. We have seen the breadth of scriptural support for that framework above.

So, on the one hand, our viewpoint is able to sit within a mainstream view of science, since it avoids any need for flood geology or any defense of why our world's animals do not look to be distributed as though they all came from a boat in Turkey around five thousand years ago. On the other hand, it can comfortably align with a high view of Scripture. This alignment does not require the dismissal of the historical timeline presented plainly in Genesis, and it avoids problematic distinctions that leave us

---

35. Longman and Walton argued first, especially from the book of Joshua, that the Bible uses hyperbole to describe historical events. They then proceeded to argue that the flood account also uses hyperbole, in a way that the original readers would have understood, on matters such as the amount of water that was involved. Longman III and Walton, *Lost World of the Flood*, 30–41.

uncertain about what events the text of Genesis is asserting as actual occurrences.

Our position has its own weaknesses. For example, it is not made clear at Gen 8:11 or thereabouts that the miracle in view was that the ark and its contents changed physical worlds. Our proposal of two distinct physical worlds can been critiqued as being science fiction. We will address such critiques at the end of the chapter. But we contend that these weaknesses are no more damaging to the overall plausibility of maintaining both a high view of Scripture and a mainstream view of science than the damage done either by Longman and Walton's approach or by those advocating that our globe was entirely flooded. But before we address the weaknesses in our proposal regarding the flood, it is worth noting some implications for our viewpoint, regarding the history of the world.

IMPLICATIONS OF OUR VIEWPOINT FOR HISTORY

Genesis 10, the chapter immediately following the flood account, is commonly referred to as the "Table of Nations." The flow of Genesis, speaking of the spread of nations immediately after the flood account, suggests that we might draw implications about the history of human nations from the nature of the flood.

How then does our viewpoint understand Genesis 10 in itself, and in its implications for human history? For those who take an approach to origins like Longman and Walton, trying to sit within a mainstream view of science, Genesis 10 is unable to be taken as a simple explanation of historical realities, because it is not viable, according to modern scientific understanding, to claim that all peoples on earth descend from Shem, Ham, and Japheth. For example, Longman and Walton's best suggestion is that the event described by the flood narrative occurred in around 5600 BC, yet the progenitors of Australia's indigenous peoples had already been in Australia for more than fifty thousand years by that time. So, if Shem, Ham, and Japheth were on a boat in 5600 BC, they could not also be the ancestors of those who lived in around 50000 BC in Australia. This rules out any traditional-style reading of Genesis 10 for Longman and Walton, where Shem, Ham, and Japheth are taken to be, in fact, the ancestors of all people alive today.

But we can ask, is it necessary to read Genesis 10 as though it teaches that all peoples are physically descended from Shem, Ham, and Japheth? We have already discussed, in chapter 2, the meaning of Acts 17:26, "From one man he made all the nations, that they should inhabit the whole earth." We suggested that the meaning reflected Gen 10:32, so that the one man was Noah, and that as Noah's descendants dispersed through existing populations, so did this political/social entity typically translated using the word "nation."

We now propose again that it is at least plausible that Gen 10:32 is teaching that a specific kind of political/social entity, a גּוֹי, "nation," spread through the dispersion of Noah's descendants, outwards from their arrival in our world on the ark. Genesis 10 does provide other categories in addition to "nations" by which we can classify people groups: לְשׁוֹן, "language";[36] מִשְׁפָּחָה, "clan";[37] מַמְלָכָה, "kingdom";[38] עִיר, "city";[39] אֶרֶץ, "territory";[40] and תּוֹלְדֹת, "descendants."[41] So, conceptually, Genesis 10 is plausibly consistent with the notion that before Noah's arrival, our world contained people across the globe existing with different languages, in clans, kingdoms, cities, and territories, and that after the flood a new social entity, the nation, spread out, through those different existing people groups steadily to the ends of the earth, through Noah's descendants.

This is not inconsistent with the possibility that an isolated nation or two, such as Egypt, existed before the time of Noah's arrival in our world. Wenham rightly argues regarding the Genesis 10 names that it is "unlikely that all the names in the list should be regarded as eponyms, i.e. the putative ancestor of the group

36. Gen 10:5.
37. Gen 10:5.
38. Gen 10:10.
39. Gen 10:12.
40. Gen 10:5, 20, 31.
41. Gen 10:32.

that bears the name."[42] This is because some of the names are place names or names of peoples, and since "sonship" and "brotherhood" could be used in ancient times to refer to a treaty relationship as well as blood-based kinship. So, there is conceptual room for the various peoples mentioned in Genesis 10 to derive some or most of their genetic stock outside of the sons of Noah. Within that framework, it remains plausible to say Genesis 10 explains that a dispersion of nations across the world occurred through the agency of Noah's descendants, a dispersion that occurred *outwards through existing populations, rather than outwards into unpopulated areas.*

For a very long time it was common to describe the indigenous people of places such as the Americas, Australia, and various islands as "peoples" or "tribes," in distinction from many people groups coming out of Europe or Asia, which were called "nations." This distinction has fallen from common usage, partly because it became associated with colonial ideas implying the superiority of nations over colonized tribes or peoples. But the changing modern use of the word "nation," changed for such reasons, does not undermine the truth that there were clear differences between the political/social organizational structures of the colonizers and the colonized.

Indeed, if we are clear about our meaning and our desire to value "nations" and "tribes" and "peoples," this language can be retained. After all, Rev 7:9 tells us that at the end of all things, there will be a multitude "from every nation, tribe, people and language, standing before the throne and before the Lamb." If tribes and peoples sit alongside nations into eternity, as seems implied here, this means that tribes, peoples, and nations must contribute in distinct and valuable ways to the glorious eternity that awaits. The real differences in socio-cultural groupings need not be removed for fear of offending those from different backgrounds. Indeed, if these differences are removed by removing the use of "tribe" or "people" from our lexicon altogether, the distinctive positive contribution of each grouping may be overlooked or undervalued.

42. Wenham, *Genesis 1–15*, 215.

But the big point does not lie in the challenge of valuing indigenous peoples with our terminology, as important as that is.
The big point regards the evidence that can be seen for Noah's
ark's arrival in our world. On that point, it remains clear that the
colonizers from the "Old World" brought a different kind of gover-
nance with them than that which existed in the "New World." Our
claim is that it is plausible that they were bringing with them a
different kind of entity, a nation, and even despite the horrors they
perpetrated in bringing nationhood across the world, still, this was
part of the ongoing way that "from one man" God "made all the
nations." This is a key part of the observable impact of Noah's ark's
arrival in our world. For Noah was that one man.

But the flood has more implications for our history than just
those regarding human dispersion. The narrative also speaks of
the animals and food brought onto the ark. So, if we understand
the story to represent historical reality, we should expect an impact
on our world that also relates to our animals and food. And so, we
turn to that question:

Gen 6:19–21 says:

> You are to bring into the ark two of all living creatures,
> male and female, to keep them alive with you. Two of ev-
> ery kind of bird, of every kind of animal and of every kind
> of creature that moves along the ground will come to you
> to be kept alive. You are to take every kind of food that is
> to be eaten and store it away as food for you and for them.

The emphasis in these verses is on the word "all," on "every"
kind. The Hebrew כֹּל, "all"/"every," appears five times in these three
verses. Noah is not to omit any of the kinds of animals or food.
Why is that? It makes sense to conclude that every kind of animal
and every kind of food was to be kept alive and stored, because
each kind had a purpose in God's plan on the other side of the
flood. So, we hypothesize that this purpose included God's desire
to bring excellent breeds of animal and strains of crop from the
pre-flood world into ours. We hypothesize that these excellent
breeds and strains were intended, among other things, to help sus-
tain human life. So, perhaps the ancient progenitors of some of our

best dairy cows, our best sheep for meat and wool, our best wheat, and so on, derive from the ark. That is not to say that there were no cows or sheep or wheat in our world before the ark arrived, but that the new arrivals helped the existing genetic stock considerably. This would be a plausible important reason to keep *every* kind of animal and food from the ancient world on the ark, and an important reason to stress that *every* kind be preserved, since every kind would have an important distinct genetic contribution to make, on the other side of the flood. Significant improvement in the genetic stock of animals is a plausible way to "keep their various kinds alive throughout the earth."[43]

As an aside, we assume that there were considerably fewer kinds of animals and food in the pre-flood world compared to ours, partly because there was room on the ark to store every kind, and also because Adam had enough time to name all the animals.[44] In this way, we can see how critiques of the flood story miss the mark when they argue that there was insufficient room in the ark for all the kinds of animals in our world. For it is plausible to suggest that the ark did not contain all the kinds of animals in our world, but only all the kinds from the pre-flood world.

It is beyond the scope of this book to test these hypotheses regarding the spread of nations and the spread of certain breeds of animal and varieties of food. However, it is noteworthy that a number of testable hypotheses may be derived from the proposals in this book, some of which will be increasingly testable as our skill in genomic testing and analysis develops.

OBJECTION 1: IS THIS JUST SCIENCE FICTION NONSENSE?

Before concluding, we now turn to two objections to our proposed timeline. One of the most common objections to this book's two-worlds timeline is to say that it is science fiction, and as such, is not

43. Gen 7:3.
44. Gen 2:19–20.

to be taken seriously. Put another way, this timeline is a parallel universe proposal of the kind that should be reserved for fictional novels, not for genuine historical discussion.

One response is to say that Christians have always believed in a physical world outside our own, one that we cannot reach with our spaceships or telescopes, no matter how good they might be. For Jesus ascended bodily into "heaven," implying that "heaven" is a place where a physical body can walk around in a physical world that is not part of our own. So, belief in the bodily ascension of Jesus implies a belief in multiple physically distinct worlds.

The notion of multiple physical worlds *with parallelisms* can be seen by thinking about God's promise to Abraham in Genesis 13. The promise is recorded this way: "The Lord said to Abram after Lot had parted from him, 'Look around from where you are, to the north and south, to the east and west. All the land that you see I will give to you and your offspring forever.'"[45] The promise of eternal inheritance is made to Abraham and his offspring. Being eternal, it is a promise of inheritance in the world to come, in Abraham's eternal home. And yet that promise says he will inherit the very land on which he was looking. So, the promise is implying that there will be, or perhaps is even now waiting, a heavenly version of that land Abraham saw.

If this is so, and such multiple yet parallel worlds are described in Genesis, then it is not implausible to suggest that Genesis might also describe Eden as existing in a place physically separate to our world, with parallel places and parallel names such as the Tigris and Euphrates Rivers.[46] Likewise, it is not implausible to suggest that Genesis might describe the pre-flood world of Noah as a world separate from our own, yet with parallel places and parallel names like Ararat.

Similar ideas have been suggested before. William Dumbrell wrote, "The Garden of Eden is thus a place separated from the outside world, which presumably is very much like our own

45. Gen 13:14–15.
46. Gen 2:14.

world."[47] His conception was to separate just the garden of Eden from us, not the whole pre-flood world, as we have proposed here. But once the former has been accepted, the latter may also be accepted without much difficulty. When Dumbrell affirmed that the garden of Eden "presumably is very much like our world," he was probably thinking of likenesses including the Tigris and Euphrates Rivers, which come together both in the Edenic world and our world. Such claims of a physically separate yet parallel world have thus been made in the past without complaints of science fiction infiltrating theology. The science fiction critique fails to take sufficient account of the nature of the Bible's claims, and the nature of historic Christian belief.

OBJECTION 2: THE NARRATIVE DOES NOT CLEARLY SAY NOAH WAS MOVED TO A DIFFERENT WORLD

Nevertheless, though there are examples like Dumbrell of describing Eden as a place separated from the outside world, challenges remain. There is the reality that the Genesis narrative does not explicitly say that Noah was moved to a different world. This is perhaps the element of this book's proposal that is the least plausible. That is, the Genesis author could have made this translation of worlds clearer by inserting text in Genesis 8 somewhere saying, "So the ark was taken from the land of God's presence and rested on Ararat," or something similar. But he did not.

Instead, after the dove brings Noah the fresh olive branch, we have the sentence, "Then Noah knew that the water had receded from the earth."[48] So, if Noah has at this point in time entered the "present heavens and earth," how can we say that the waters have *receded*, if they never covered our earth? How can this be said *after* he received the fresh olive branch, if the only place to get a fresh olive branch is now in our world?

47. Dumbrell, *Faith of Israel*, 19.
48. Gen 8:11.

We suggest it is plausible that God sees the "earth" of the ancient world as being so connected to our earth that he doesn't see the need to distinguish the two worlds clearly. This is similar to the way God tells Abraham that he will inherit "all the land that you see,"[49] when in fact Abraham will receive that land in the "new heavens and earth," not in our world, at least not in the way we would normally speak of "our world."

Moreover, note that the verb קלל, translated in Gen 8:11 as "receded" in the NIV, literally means "to be small" or "to be insignificant," and is rendered in the perfect tense in Gen 8:11. So, a more literal translation of the phrase would be, "then Noah observed that the water was insignificant upon the earth." This allows for any significant recession of the water to have occurred before the dove fetched the olive leaf, and with no significant recession afterward. The perfect tense of "was insignificant"[50] carries a perfective aspect that views the situation as an "undifferentiated whole,"[51] from a distant perspective, rather than viewing the progressive nature of the situation. So, in Gen 8:11 there is no sense communicated of Noah observing the waters receding after he received the olive branch, but rather of the final state, when the waters were of little note.

In Gen 8:13, again, the perfect tense is used to express the water having dried up from the earth: "By the first day of the first month of Noah's six hundred and first year, the water was dried up." The choice of the perfect tense for the verb חָרְבוּ, "was dried up," emphasizes the end result of it being dried, rather than the process of it drying. That is, Genesis does not teach that after receiving the olive leaf, Noah saw the water receding. So, it is possible that there was either no flood in our world, or a limited body of water somewhere in the mountains of Ararat, when the ark appeared in our world. We can acknowledge that this is still the least plausible element of this book's proposal. Nonetheless, we maintain that the

49. Gen 13:15.
50. Patton and Putnam, *Hebrew Discourse*, 62.
51. Patton and Putnam, *Hebrew Discourse*, 62.

overall evidence supporting this book's timeline makes it no less plausible than the published alternatives. It is time to conclude.

CONCLUSION

In this chapter, we have interacted with two noteworthy positions on the historical character of the Genesis flood narrative. The first is the traditional view that our whole globe was flooded. The second is Longman and Walton's view that while Genesis's *interpretations* of the flood event and ancient flood traditions may be taken as authoritative, its *descriptions* may not.

We have contended that our position is at least as plausible as those that claim our whole globe was flooded, because the scientific claims necessary to defend that thesis, with "flood geology" and the like, are at least as speculative as the most speculative claims we have made.

We have also contended that our position is at least as plausible as Longman and Walton's because we have explained in more detail than they what the text of Genesis 6–9 means, with more attention to the details of the text. The connections we have drawn between the Genesis text itself and the history behind it are more plausible than theirs because ours are more straightforward and leave us with a more satisfactory doctrine of Scripture.

We have seen that our position's weaknesses, such as the omission of a clear point of the ark's transfer into our world, and the allegedly science-fictional nature of the proposal, have responses that are sufficiently plausible to make our position overall no less plausible than Longman and Walton's, even given that parts of our proposal might be described as "strange."

In our next chapter, we will consider Genesis's account of the Tower of Babel, and how our book's timeline understands it, such that it can be embraced historically, without implying that there was only one language in the world as recently as 4,500 years ago. This will add further plausibility to our own timeline, especially when compared to other major alternatives.

Chapter 5

The Tower of Babel

INTRODUCTION

IN OUR OPENING CHAPTER, we outlined challenges integrating the early parts of Genesis with mainstream scientific and historical perspectives. In the chapters that followed, we have explored potential solutions to these challenges, through explaining our two-worlds thesis and its associated timeline. It remains now to address the integrative challenges presented by the Tower of Babel account in Gen 11:1–9.

There are several potential approaches to this task. We might consider the biblical date of the tower, its location, the language spoken by the people at the tower, or the archaeological evidence for such a tower's existence. The most challenging integrative aspect of the story, however, is its reference to a "language of the whole world."[1] This biblical notion of the existence of such a language as late as the third millennium BC seems to conflict squarely with the mainstream position that there was no such singular world language. The main burden of this chapter is to propose a plausible

1. Gen 11:9.

solution to this integrative challenge. We will seek to do so using our two-worlds thesis, arguing that the language described by Gen 11:1–9 was plausibly the sole language of the once-cursed world, but never the sole language of our twice-cursed world.

So, the chapter will argue that the tower account plausibly depicts a group comprising people sourced from the once-cursed world. These descendants of Adam sought to make a name for themselves among other people in the twice-cursed world. This case will be made by considering evidence within the text for the existence of these two distinct groups. We will make the case that when the Genesis account is read this way, the Sumerian language and people group fit well as the historical referent of the story. Finally, we will seek to counter a claim made by biblical scholar and theologian Peter Enns. Enns argued that the existence of Mesopotamian parallel language versions of Genesis's earliest stories rules out any potential contribution Genesis might make to modern debates about human origins.

WHO THE TOWER OF BABEL ACCOUNT IS ABOUT

Identifying who the narrative is about in the Tower of Babel account presents a problem. Genesis 11:1 states that "all the land" had "one language and the same words." Then in verse 2 the narrative tells us that "they" moved eastward and found a plain in Shinar. The NIV translates this verse, "[a]s *people* moved eastward and found a plain in Shinar . . . ," but the word "people" is an addition by the translator. So, who is the passage about? Given that the people in the account want to "make a name"[2] for themselves, it seems unlikely that *all people in existence* are in view. It makes more sense to conclude that the people being referenced want to make a name for themselves among others, rather than among themselves. After all, the drive for fame typically involves seeking recognition from an external entity, rather than a group seeking fame among its own members.

2. Gen 11:4.

Hamilton suggested that it is the *builders* of the tower who are trying to make a name for themselves.[3] This at least provides an in-group and an out-group, so we could suggest the builders are trying to make a name for themselves among the non-builders.

But if it is just the builders in view, their group identity seems very odd, for builders' unions are not typically the kind concerned "that they will be scattered over the face of the whole earth."[4] More than that, God himself, when speaking about the group, says, "If as *one people speaking the same language*, they have begun to do this,"[5] so when God identifies the group, he does so by speaking of them as a single people with a single language. Additionally, if it were just the builders who were to blame for the tower project, it would not seem fitting that their punishment be applied to the whole people, nor to their whole language. So, it seems quite un-likely that the group in question throughout the passage could be simply the builders of the tower.

This leads us to propose an alternative understanding, one that extends what we saw in chapter 2. In that chapter, we saw that Cain very likely found people not descended from Adam in his place of banishment. So, likewise, we can propose the existence of two similarly structured groups in the tower story. The group building the tower could plausibly be comprised of biological de-scendants of Adam, while the group among whom they want to make a name could plausibly be people not descended from Adam.

The plausibility of this suggestion is strengthened by noting that in verse 5 the people are called בְּנֵי הָאָדָם, literally "sons of the Adam." While this phrase is used sixteen times in the Hebrew Bible, mostly in Ecclesiastes, to speak of "mankind," this is its only use in the Torah. Given such a rare usage in this part of the Bible, it is plausible that this construction is designed to make the reader consider that this subgroup might indeed be the biological descendants of Adam, a group to be differentiated from the kinds of people Cain found when he was banished. This suggestion, in

3. Hamilton, *Genesis 1–17*, 353–54.

4. Gen 11:4.

5. Gen 11:6.

turn, gives us more to say about the language being spoken in the account.

THE LANGUAGE OF THE WHOLE WORLD

The opening sentence of the Tower of Babel account tells us, literally, that כָל־הָאָרֶץ, "all the land," had "one language and the same words." Verse 2 then continues, "As people moved eastward, they found a plain in Shinar." Both 11:1 and 11:2 begin with the special verb וַיְהִי, sometimes translated in older versions as "and it came to pass."[6] The double usage of this verb is unusual enough that Wenham notes it, comparing it with Gen 4:2b–3 to claim that such usage is a distinctive of the primeval history.[7] While traditionally translated "and it came to pass," modern scholarship enables us to be more precise about its meaning. וַיְהִי can introduce a new unit, as it does in Gen 11:1. But it can also move the narrative timeframe to a new point.[8] If we take such usage to apply in Gen 11:2, we can understand the passage as follows: Verse 1 supplies the background setting, the setting that applied in the once-cursed land of Adam through to Noah. In that land, there was one language, and the same words. Methuselah and all the others never had any translation problems, as they lived their extended lifespans. They all spoke the same language, in that pre-flood world, until their world was deluged and destroyed. That is the background communicated in Genesis 11:1.

The use of וַיְהִי at the start of verse 2 moves the narrative timeframe to a new point in time, a much later time. We can assume that, through Cain's descendants and Noah's descendants, this original language of the once-cursed world continued to be spoken in the twice-cursed world, but not now by everyone. So, our attention in the narrative has turned to a group of people who spoke that original language, now in a world where most did not.

6. See Gen 11:2 in the KJV, for example.

7. Wenham, *Genesis 1–15*, 234.

8. For discussion of the uses of וַיְהִי in Hebrew narrative, see Patton and Putnam, *Hebrew Discourse*, 71.

THE TOWER OF BABEL

They were journeying eastward, looking for a place to settle. We have jumped into this new timeframe in order that we might hear the story of the demise of that original human language.

For such a reading to make sense, we need to understand Gen 11:9 as follows: "That is why it was called Babel—because there the Lord confused *what had been* the language of the whole land." The context just described, and all the work we have done so far in this book, serves to make this understanding plausible.

FURTHER STRENGTHS OF OUR UNDERSTANDING OF THE TOWER ACCOUNT

A further strength of this understanding of the tower story is seen in its clarity regarding where the people went wrong. With our understanding of the passage, we can clearly explain the text's criticism of the people seeking to "make a name"[9] for themselves. That is, their sin is that they seek to stay together and build the tower *primarily* in order to make a name for themselves amongst the other people around them. They do not want to be "scattered over the face of the whole earth,"[10] in particular because in that case *their people and language group* would not be exalted above the other peoples and language groups. The problem is their goal of seeking to make a name for themselves and thus raising their status above that of other people groups. This building project does not seek to serve others in any way, either God or other people, but seeks only to exalt this people group at the expense of others, and that is the problem. But notice that the problem can only be defined that way if we acknowledge the existence of other people groups.

Examples of similar sins today could be seen if someone's approach to social media has the primary goal that they become famous while not caring how that happens, or if a nation seeks to be great compared to other nations, as a primary end in itself. Perhaps the goal of landing humanity on Mars might be defensible

9. Gen 11:4.
10. Gen 11:4.

generically, but the tower story implies that it is not defensible if one nation is seeking to do it primarily to make a name for themselves among the other nations.

In this context, God's acknowledgement that "nothing they plan to do will be impossible for them" does not mean they will be able to do literally anything, but rather that as things stand, this people group will be able to be endlessly successful *in this goal of setting themselves over other peoples*. God does not want one people subjugating all the others, which is where this impetus will head, so he must put a stop to it.

But notice that without this clear notion that there are other peoples in existence among whom this people were trying to make a name, commentators have lacked clarity in diagnosing the sin. So, commentator Bruce Waltke wrote that the account "reveals the formerly unified people building a tower in collective, titanic rebellion against God."[11] Yes, that is fair in a way, in that all sin is at heart rebellion against God. But Waltke pressed this as the key characteristic of *this sin*, because he had no out-group of humans he could point to, among whom the people were trying to make a name. So, for Waltke, God is the only candidate over and against whom the people might have been trying to make their name great, and that is why he overemphasized the character of this sin as titanic rebellion against God.

Again, Genesis commentator Robert Alter wrote that "the polemic thrust of the story is against urbanism and the overweening confidence of humanity in the feats of technology."[12] Without the existence of a human out-group over whom the people were exalting themselves, Alter was casting around trying to find, concretely, the heart of the sin involved. But he missed the mark. Urbanism is not the heart of the problem, but urbanism *if it is pursued primarily in order to exalt one's own people group over others*. Confidence in the feats of technology is not the heart of the problem, but pursuing technology *primarily in order to exalt one's own people group over others* is the issue. It is at the very least plausible

11. Waltke and Fredricks, *Genesis*, 161.
12. Alter, *Hebrew Bible*, 1:38.

that commentators have struggled to point precisely to the nature of the sin at the Tower of Babel, because they have not embraced the notion that there was an out-group among whom the people were trying to make a name. The more this is accepted, the more plausible our two-world thesis becomes.

One last strength of our thesis is worth mentioning before we seek to identify the language scattered at Babel: The current ordering of Genesis 10–11 has been the subject of debate, with some commentators arguing that it does not reflect the correct chronological order of events. So, Longman wrote, "Genesis 10 must follow Genesis 11:1–9 temporally because Genesis 10 describes the world broken up into language groups."[13] His point is grounded in his assumption that Genesis is communicating that there were no other language groups in existence at the time of the Tower of Babel account. He was arguing that if Genesis 10 has multiple depicted languages, which it does, it must come temporally after Genesis 11, which does not have multiple languages, according to Longman's understanding. But if, with our thesis, we acknowledge multiple languages at the time of the Babel account, we do not have to conclude that these chapters are temporally out of order.

At the least, then, our approach opens more flexibility for conclusions about the temporal relationship between the chapters, giving us more reasons to endorse the final editor's decision regarding the order of the chapters. This additional flexibility enhances the plausibility of our two-worlds thesis.

THE LANGUAGE WAS LIKELY SUMERIAN

With that, we have reached a point where we can seek to identify the historical setting for this language, the language in view in the tower account of Gen 11:1–9. A number of factors point to it being the Sumerian language. We will explore seven lines of argument that this is the case, lines of argument that in many places depend on a two-worlds understanding of the narrative.

13. Longman III, *Genesis*, 151.

In the first place, the only ancient Mesopotamian text with potential parallels to the biblical tower story is a Sumerian-language
epic called "Enmerkar and the Lord of Aratta."[14] S. N. Kramer and
S. Cohen translated the key lines of that text as follows:

> Enki . . . the leader of the gods
> changed the speech in their mouths
> brought contention into it,
> Into the speech of man that (until then) had been one.[15]

Kramer himself concluded that this text "puts it beyond
all doubt that the Sumerians believed there was a time when all
mankind spoke one and the same language."[16] Others disagree and
understand this passage to look forward to a time when all will
one day speak the same language.[17] Resolving this debate is complicated and beyond this author. But either way, this is the leading
plausible parallel to the Genesis story from ancient Mesopotamian
sources, and it was written in Sumerian, and about the Sumerian
language. It is plausible then to suggest that the reason the only
parallel to the biblical tower account is in Sumerian is that Sumerian is the language the story is about. It is plausible to suggest that
the reason the Sumerians uniquely claimed to have once spoken
the sole language of the whole world is that they did, albeit in a
world physically separate from our own.

A second reason to suggest that the tower account is about
the Sumerian language is the use of the place name שִׁנְעָר, "Shinar,"
in Gen 11:2. Hamilton wrote, "Shinar undoubtedly represents
the land of Mesopotamia, a territory that was first called Sumer,
then Sumer and Akkad, and then Babylonia. Why 'Sumer' should
appear as 'Shinar' is not clear." He provides the suggestion taken
from A. Poebel that the Hebrew word is taken from Sumerian,
and represents a word "the Sumerians used to express the idea of

---

14. Wenham, *Genesis 1–15*, 236.

15. Wenham, *Genesis 1–15*, 236.

16. Kramer, "Babel of Tongues," 108–11.

17. Alster, "Aratta," 101–9.

Babylonia as a whole."[18] It is plausible then to say that since the biblical text uses a Sumerian word to express the setting of the story within the area that was once called Sumer, Sumerian should be the leading candidate for the language the passage is describing.

A third reason to favor the conclusion that the language behind the Genesis 11 account is Sumerian is that the oldest accounts of the great flood, with striking similarities to the biblical account, were written in the Sumerian language.[19] These include *Eridu Genesis*, as well as the Sumerian King List. The latter mirrors the biblical account in that it acknowledges that there was a great flood and records the lifespan of the pre-flood kings to have been far in excess of those after the flood. The point is that it is plausible to suggest that the earliest versions of the flood story were written in the language of those who experienced it. Given that the earliest versions are in Sumerian, it is plausible to believe that Noah and his sons spoke Sumerian, as did their descendants up until and including those at the Tower of Babel, where that language was finally confused.

A fourth observation, consistent with the theory that the language confused at Babel was Sumerian, is the strong likelihood that the earliest writing we possess is in the Sumerian language.[20] If indeed it is the case that the Sumerian language/people group were the ones of whom God particularly thought, "nothing they plan will be impossible for them,"[21] because they had the advantages of being descended from Adam, including extended lifespan effects that lingered even after exiting the once-cursed world, then we should expect these people to produce many early key inventions. This is consistent with them being the inventors of the first system of writing. The Sumerians produced many other key early inventions, such as the most ancient collection of laws in the world.[22]

18. Hamilton, *Genesis 1–17*, 351; Poebel, "Name of Elam," 26.

19. For a list of similarities between the Genesis account and the main Mesopotamian parallels, see Enns, *Evolution of Adam*, 46.

20. Roux, *Ancient Iraq*, 75.

21. Gen 11:6.

22. Roux, *Ancient Iraq*, 162.

A fifth reason to conclude that the language scattered at Babel was plausibly Sumerian involves connecting the biblical tower account with the physical structures widely understood to be described there, the Mesopotamian ziggurats.[23] We can look in history for a ziggurat built in southern Mesopotamia at the time the Bible suggests for the event, and see what language the builders most likely spoke. Regarding the time period in question, Gen 10:25 tells us that "in [Peleg's] time the earth was divided." Many have taken this to provide the Bible's dating for the Tower of Babel events. Wenham made this connection, noting that the verb in question, פלג, "to divide," can be used of speech being confused.[24]

In the appendix to this book, the calculation is given for the dates of Peleg's birth and death, yielding the range 2372–2033 BC. This must be taken as a rough estimate, since a number of key decisions change the result significantly. Taking the earliest plausible date for his birth and the latest for his death,[25] "Peleg's time" could sit anywhere between c. 2780–1720 BC. The fact that his father Eber outlived him makes it curious that Peleg, rather than Eber, was selected to mark the time of the world's division, and this makes it more likely that "Peleg's time" might refer specifically to the time leading up to his death, roughly 2033 BC on our best estimate.

The Sumerian speakers were building ziggurats at roughly that time in southern Mesopotamia. So, for example, on the Middle chronology,[26] Ur-Nammu reigned 2112–2094 BC, which would

23. Georges Roux, for example, connects the Mesopotamian ziggurats to the story of the Tower of Babel. See Roux, *Ancient Iraq*, 163–65.

24. Wenham, *Genesis 1–15*, 231. He cites Ps 55:9 as an example of the verb being used in that fashion.

25. The late date here involves taking the MT version of the text, the shorter stay in Egypt, and 300 years between the exodus and the temple. The early date involves taking the LXX version of the text, the longer stay in Egypt, and 480 years between the exodus and the temple. See the appendix for details.

26. For a classical overview of the discussion of the low, middle, and high chronology of Mesopotamia, see Brinkman, "Appendix: Mesopotamian Chronology," 335–48. The difference between the ultra-low chronology and the high chronology is 152 years. The middle chronology is the one typically cited.

plausibly place him within "Peleg's time,"[27] since Peleg's death is the next death of the biblical patriarchs after that reign. Ur-Nammu was a Sumerian king, whom Roux describes as "for ever associated with the *ziqqurats* . . . which he erected in Ur, Uruk, Eridu, Nipur and various other cities."[28] The point is that the Sumerian ziggurat building history makes Sumerian a very plausible candidate for the language of those who built the Tower of Babel.

A sixth reason to propose that the language confused at Babel was Sumerian is this: that Sumerian ceased to be a spoken language soon after Ur-Nammu's extensive ziggurat building program. The Sumerian nation and type of society also ended around this time. Roux put it this way:

> The fall of Ur at the close of the third millennium B.C. is one of the major turning-points in the history of ancient Iraq: it does not only ring the knell of a dynasty and of an empire, it marks the end of the Sumerian nation and type of society . . . Even before Ur was captured, the Sumerian empire had collapsed, and Mesopotamia had been shattered into a mosaic of large or small kingdoms, the most important being those of Isin and Larsa in the south, Assur and Eshunna in the north . . . The rulers who replaced the Sumerians on the political stage were either Akkadians from Iraq or Western Semites—'Amorites' in the broad sense of the term—from Syria and the western desert . . . As they spoke Semitic dialects they adopted in writing the Akkadian language, and slowly in the south, rapidly in the north, the latter prevailed over Sumerian in private and official inscriptions . . . [It was a] linguistic revolution.[29]

That is to say, Sumerian was plausibly a language that was confused, and their people scattered, shortly after a time when they had built a number of towers that we call "ziggurats," which fit the description of the Tower of Babel. This all plausibly occurred

27. See the appendix for details.
28. Roux, *Ancient Iraq*, 163.
29. Roux, *Ancient Iraq*, 180.

at a date that may be called the "time of Peleg," that is, according to the biblical timeline for the Tower of Babel.

A seventh reason to conclude that the language of the Tower of Babel account was Sumerian is the following: that just as the biblical account presents the people in the story as a people defined by their language, so it was with the Sumerians. In Gen 11:6, God describes the people as "one people speaking the same language." Roux described the Sumerian people similarly: "Stricto sensu, the appellation 'Sumerians' should be taken as meaning 'Sumerian-speaking people' and nothing else."[30] This is not a characteristic typically ascribed to a people, and so the nature of this description increases the plausibility that the Tower of Babel account is describing the Sumerian people and language.

When we consider all seven pieces of evidence together, it becomes not only plausible, but likely, that the Tower of Babel account is describing the decline of the Sumerian language and the dispersion of its speakers.

However, accepting this historical setting for the tower account also requires accepting the two-worlds thesis and timeline presented in this book. That is to say, we know in our world that Sumerian was at no point the sole language. Yet in Genesis 11, the language in question is described as "the language of the whole world." So, it seems impossible to identify the language of Genesis 11 with the Sumerian language without our proposal that there was a separate physical world in which this was the sole language. The fact that this interpretation aligns so well with the evidence, where traditional readings fail to provide a viable historical integration, strengthens the case for taking the two-worlds thesis and timeline of this book seriously.

But that brings us to the question of whether it is appropriate to look for historical referents for these early Genesis narratives at all. We conclude this chapter by looking at Peter Enns's arguments that no such historical referents should be sought.

---

30. Roux, *Ancient Iraq*, 81.

ENNS'S CASE AGAINST GENESIS'S RELEVANCE IN THE HUMAN ORIGINS DEBATE

In his book *The Evolution of Adam*, Peter Enns made an extended case that we should not expect the early chapters of Genesis to contribute to contemporary scientific or historical debates about human origins.

To make his case, he first pointed out various similarities between the *Atrahasis Epic* and Genesis, concluding that "The general storyline of *Atrahasis* is similar to Genesis 2–8 as a whole: creation, population growth, flood."[31] He then moved to his conclusion using the following argument:

> Whether or not Genesis is actually modelled after *Atrahasis* deliberately, there is no question that they share a common way of describing the primordial world. Seeing the similarities between these two stories should discourage us from expecting the Adam story to contribute to contemporary debates about human origins (let alone guide those debates). Likewise, the similarities between Genesis and *Atrahasis* suggest that the biblical account cannot be labelled "historical," at least not in any conventional sense of the word . . . Genesis 1 speaks of the instantaneous creation of mankind . . . humans, along with every other form of life, are created "according to its kind"—no development from one species to another. This biblical view cannot in any way be joined to modern scientific models.[32]

One of the problems with such sweeping statements about science and history is that the claims are oversimplified. Such sweeping claims rule out a number of possibilities, without working hard enough to justify the conclusion.

For example, if a dual biological creation of humanity is the reality, so that humans were created both through special creation and also through an evolutionary route, and if hints of this are there in the scriptural accounts, then the Scriptures do have

31. Enns, *Evolution of Adam*, 52.
32. Enns, *Evolution of Adam*, 53.

something to contribute to scientific endeavor: they can push scientists to consider what evidence there might be that humans did have such origins, and posit hypotheses accordingly.

Or again, if evolved biological humans, together at a certain point in time, across the planet, received, in miraculous fashion, a human soul, around seven thousand years ago, and if this changed their behavior substantially, and if the Scriptures give hints as to the point in time that this occurred, then the Scriptures do have a contribution to make to scientific endeavor. They can push scientists to consider what evidence there might be that this were the case and posit hypotheses accordingly.

Again, if a small number of theological humans appeared in our world miraculously, speaking a new language we now call Sumerian, and had an enormous impact on world history, and if significant hints of this are to be found in the Scriptures, then the Scriptures do have something important to contribute to our understanding of human origins. They can push historians to consider what they should expect to see in history, were this in fact the character of the origin of the Sumerian language and people.

It is true that these ancient Mesopotamian myths have parallels to the Bible, as well as depicting clear falsehoods. They depict false realities such as a polytheistic set of gods or a dome holding up waters in our sky, in the midst of their creation stories that parallel the Bible's. However, these observations alone are not sufficient to conclude that there are errors in Genesis. It remains possible that Genesis could be picking up elements of the Mesopotamian myths that are true, and leaving behind elements that are not.

So, we may plausibly propose that the Mesopotamian stories captured some truth, through their proximity to the actual events, while also expressing their own errors, errors that sprang from their worship of false gods and syncretism and more besides. The Sumerian King List might indeed capture the fact that there were very long-lived individuals before the great flood, but the passage of time may have caused that list to overstate the length of lives. The Sumerian storytellers might have remembered that there was a firmament holding up a torrent of water, in the once-cursed world, and falsely assumed that our twice-cursed world must be the same. There are many plausible avenues open that allow us to suggest that while the ancient Mesopotamian myths are older than the biblical accounts, and have parallels to the biblical stories, and have clear errors, that this need not imply the biblical accounts must also contain errors. Enns is right that those ancient Mesopotamian manuscripts have important implications for the Bible, but his sweeping conclusions are not justified.

Those with a high view of Scripture can still maintain that God, through his Spirit, passed on to Moses and others the true history of these events, and enabled them to be recorded accurately for our benefit. Therefore, despite there being errors in ancient Mesopotamian texts, and despite those texts having clear parallels with the Genesis accounts, the conjunction of these two facts is insufficient to conclude that the Bible has nothing to contribute to the history or the science of origins.

CONCLUSION

Let us now draw the arguments of this chapter together. The chapter has focussed on the Tower of Babel account of Gen 11:1–9. We have seen that the people described there were not likely to be the only people in existence at the time, because they wanted to make a name for themselves, and the character of such activity implies the existence of people outside of the group, among whom the name is to be made. We have seen the plausibility of the claim that this group were the descendants of Adam, trying to make a name for themselves among the people who were not descended from Adam. We have seen the ways in which this claim enables greater precision regarding the nature of the sin committed in the building of the Tower of Babel.

We also canvased seven reasons to conclude that Sumerian is the language confused at Babel. These included the fact that the only ancient parallel to the Tower of Babel is a Sumerian-language story; the fact that Gen 11:2 mentions a place name that likely means "Sumer"; the fact that the oldest accounts of the great flood are in the Sumerian language, as well as the oldest writing; the fact that the ziggurat structures were built by the Sumerians at the relevant time and place that the Bible describes; the decline of the Sumerian language matching the timeframe the Bible describes; and the tight link between the Sumerian language and people, paralleling the biblical account of the Tower of Babel. We have seen that the ability to make this link to the Sumerian language with such strong supporting evidence increases the plausibility of our two-worlds thesis, since many of these points can only be made within that framework.

We concluded by noting there is no need to follow Enns in rejecting Genesis's potential to contribute to modern debates on human origins merely because parallel accounts to the Genesis material have errors. Rather, we can maintain that all the Scriptures have told the truth by the Spirit's power, and that Mesopotamian parallel stories are to be expected because of the shared history involved.

It remains now to draw the arguments of this book to a conclusion.

Chapter 6

Conclusion

THIS BOOK'S PROPOSAL PUT SIMPLY

As we conclude, it is useful to express this book's proposal simply. If we have just a few paragraphs to do so, we would say the following:

It makes sense to say that the garden of Eden was a different physical world from ours. It was a perfect world, so there would be no lightning strikes or earthquakes or annoying animals like mosquitoes. That means it had to be a physically separate world from ours, so that our world would not infect theirs. Many people say something like that.

Our new hypothesis is that after the fall, Adam and Eve were *still* in a physically separate world from ours. So, it was only cherubim and a flaming sword stopping them going back to the tree of life, which meant they had not been moved to an entirely different physical setting. But when Cain was punished for killing Abel, he was cast by God somewhere very different. In his new world, Cain was afraid of being killed, not of being lonely. That is what you would expect if he found lots of strangers in his new place, rather than nobody at all until his yet-to-be-born siblings grew up.

So, we propose that Cain was cast into our world. He found a wife to marry and people to form a city, in our world. Our world is harder to farm than Adam and Eve's, since ours sits under both the curse on Adam and the curse on Cain, whereas theirs only ever saw Adam's curse. So, Noah's flood was not a flood of our world, but it was a flood that destroyed the world from which Cain had been banished. That is, it destroyed the world that contained both Eden and the places outside Eden where Cain and Abel had lived together.

How plausible have we found this proposal to be? We will now review some key points relevant to our proposal's overall plausibility, before considering its plausibility relative to competing theories.

OVERALL PLAUSIBILITY

This book's major strengths include the following: Firstly, the argument is strong that Genesis intends a timeline to be calculated from the data of its relevant genealogies, since precisely the necessary data is provided by Genesis, and since even if there are men omitted in those genealogies, the timeline remains unchanged. Secondly, the argument is strong that after his banishment, Cain's fear of being killed, rather than his fear of loneliness, points to unrelated new people being in his new location. Thirdly, the notion that the flood destroyed the world Cain left behind, rather than our own world, has the strength that it allows us to avoid saying our world was completely flooded, and so we avoid having to defend associated propositions that clash fundamentally with mainstream science. Fourthly, it is a strength that our proposed timeline does not place full humans at any stage alongside any species of *Homo* that were not in God's image, thus avoiding moral questions of how humans were meant to treat such beings. Fifthly, it is a strength that on our timeline and assumption set, we are uniquely able to identify a plausible historical context for the Tower of Babel account. This connection is established through the observation that the Sumerian language was the language of the most significant ancient ziggurat builders, who constructed their ziggurats in the geographical and temporal context indicated by Genesis for the Tower of Babel.

The biggest reasons a reader might dismiss this book's core proposals include the following: Firstly, our hypothesis that all biological *Homo sapiens* in our world received a human soul simultaneously, to make them fully human, around seven thousand years ago, will be seen by many as implausible. On the one hand, many will see it as too interventionist on God's part to be a proposal sitting within mainstream science, while others will note such a claim is not specifically mentioned in Scripture, making it speculative. Secondly, the notion that not only Eden, but the whole pre-flood world might have been physically distinct from our own will be seen by many as implausible. Many will likely dismiss such a hypothesis as the stuff of science fiction parallel universes, inherently implausible. Thirdly, many will find our hypothesis of a miraculous translation of Noah's ark from the world of that time to our world not only implausible in itself, but also absent from the biblical text. The word translated "behold" in Gen 8:11 might well point to a miracle, but it will be seen as implausible to take that miracle to be a "translation" of the ark and its inhabitants between worlds, with no clarity about how much water came from one world to another as the ark landed in ours. Fourthly, many will consider it implausible that non-theological-human *Homo sapiens* could produce such wonders as complex symbolic cave art, carved images, and other achievements that have been discovered and dated ten thousand years ago or earlier in our world. Fifthly and finally, many will consider this whole book's attempt to integrate biblical texts with the conclusions of mainstream science inherently implausible, due to the nature of the biblical texts.

In weighing the overall plausibility of our proposals, then, part of the job is to weigh the strength of the first list against the strength of the second. It is our claim that we have done enough through the chapters of this book to tip the balance in favor of the overall plausibility of the proposal. Some of the most important points we have made in mitigating against perceived weaknesses are as follows:

The objection to suggesting a worldwide simultaneous bestowal of full humanity to non-human *Homo sapiens* was addressed as follows: we argued that our theory resolves a dilemma faced by mainstream writers who propose that our ancestors were still evolving essential human traits and characteristics after approximately 60000 BC in Europe or Africa. When such writers make these claims, they run the risk of implying that these traits or characteristics developed after the migration of those who eventually became the indigenous peoples of Australia, thus potentially undermining their fundamental humanity in theoretical terms. This book's proposals avoid this conclusion in the clearest possible manner: through a global interventionist act of God that bestows full theological humanity upon all *Homo sapiens*, regardless of how geographically dispersed they were at that point in history.

We also offered a plausible defense for the notion that the first full theological humans might be dated to well after our best dating of the first cave art and other symbolic or ritualistic behaviors. Our defense included two key points. Firstly, we suggested that some abilities commensurate with these artistic and ritualistic achievements could plausibly be attributed to Neanderthals, even though they are typically not categorized as human in any sense. Secondly, we noted that the range of behaviors we attribute to animals has been historically underestimated, and that this underestimation may persist.

The objection that our separate world hypothesis for Eden and surrounds is science fiction parallel universe nonsense was met by pointing out that Jesus now lives in a physically separate world from us, in his physical body, and this is not seen by Christians as science fiction nonsense. Similarly, the notion that Abraham is looking forward to receiving the very land he looked on, in a future heavenly land, is not generally seen as parallel universe nonsense by those with a high view of Scripture, despite it endorsing a reality that could be described as a parallel universe.

Lastly, we pointed out that a miraculous translation of the ark from the world of that time to our world seems *less miraculous* than the alternative traditional proposal that all tree and plant life globally survived 150 days under kilometers of water.

All told, with weaknesses mitigated and strengths underlined, it is our claim that we have presented a timeline and explanation of human origins that plausibly integrates a high view of Scripture and a mainstream view of science. But it is one thing to claim that overall plausibility has been demonstrated, and another to claim that our timeline is at least as compelling as others in its explanatory power. So, we turn now to consider that question.

COMPARATIVE PLAUSIBILITY: THE TRADITIONAL VIEW

Our aim now is to draw conclusions about this book's plausibility *relative* to other major treatments of the subject. To do this, we will focus on two alternative approaches that seek to integrate Scripture and science/history *from within a high view of Scripture.* So, we are asking: from within a high view of Scripture, when both strengths and weaknesses of different positions are weighed, and when a position must be chosen, how strong does this book's position look?

We begin with the traditional view, which we take to include at least the following aspects: It accepts that a timeline may be constructed from the genealogies of Genesis. It embraces the notion that our whole world was flooded, with all modern humans and animals descended from those who exited the ark, which they did around five thousand years ago. It also claims that the Tower of Babel story is historical, describing the confusion of a language that until then had been the only language of the world.

Adherents of this view would likely see this book's weaknesses as including the speculative nature of the thesis that God used Adam's post-fall soul as a model or source for human souls, which he then bestowed globally on existing *Homo sapiens* to bring them into their full humanity. They would likely find fault with the speculative nature of Noah's ark's translation from one world to another as the miracle implied in Gen 8:11. They would likely critique as speculative special pleading our reading of Genesis 11, where we understand it to say that at Babel the language dispersed *had once been* the language of all the earth. Above all, they would likely stress that our whole set of proposals is driven more by a desire to align with the scientific world's evolutionary theories than with Scripture.

In response, we contend that the list of implausibilities they must accept is at least as troublesome as those associated with this book. They have the real challenge of explaining where all the water of the flood came from and where it went if it covered even the mountains of Ararat, let alone Mount Everest. They have to explain why the distribution of animals and humans in our world looks nothing like it should if all modern-day animals and humans came from an ark in modern-day Turkey. Without a proposal like our reading of Gen 11:1, with the two-worlds thesis necessarily attached, the claim that there was once a sole language of the world, scattered at Babel, on the timeline implied by the Genesis genealogies is indefensible on mainstream scientific assumptions. It requires, for example, telling indigenous Australians that their ancestors were not in Australia before c. 2900 BC, and that their language descends directly from a Mesopotamian language spoken at about that time.

To respond to these challenges, those of the traditional view have propagated a host of speculative proposals, both in scientific terms and in biblical terms. In terms of the Bible, they have argued against the notion that Cain met people unrelated to him in the world of his banishment. To do this, they seem compelled to argue that unmentioned brothers or sisters of Cain had by the time of Abel's death already grown to the age where they might threaten Cain, so that Cain was scared of them. This is speculative, albeit a fairly mainstream kind of speculation. But it is not nearly so speculative as all the pseudo-scientific attempts they need to make to explain how our world experienced a global flood five thousand or so years ago when mainstream scientists have so many grounds to deny the same. When all the speculation contained in flood geology and its ilk is considered, the speculations of traditionalists are at least as pronounced as those associated with this book's thesis. So, it is fitting to conclude that our book's proposals are at least as plausible as those of the traditionalists for integrating Genesis 1–11 with history and science.

COMPARATIVE PLAUSIBILITY: CRAIG, LONGMAN, WALTON AND SWAMIDASS

We turn then to the other major comprehensive integrative theory of early Genesis and science/history. We call it a single theory because although the different authors represented would quibble with each other at points, on the grand scale, they are sufficiently alike to be taken together. We have interacted with important modern representatives of this viewpoint, notably Craig, Swamidass, Longman and Walton, and so we ascribe this viewpoint to their names, though many others hold it. This viewpoint is characterized first by a high view of Scripture. It is a viewpoint that is typically open to, if not embracing outright, the notion that *Adam was a historical figure who evolved, rather than being formed from dust.* Adherents of this viewpoint see the historical event behind the flood story as a *localized* flood in our world. They reject the notion that a timeline can be constructed from the Genesis genealogy data, and they deny that actual historical events can be simply read from the text of Genesis 1–11.

Adherents of this viewpoint will likely agree with the traditionalists that this book's thesis is too speculative at key points, and is unsupported by clear scriptural backing. They are also likely to make the critique that ancient cave art and religious activity of hominids proves that humans existed in our world well before 5100 BC. So, they are likely to depict this book's position as standing for that reason outside of mainstream science. Taking more stock than traditionalists do of the mainstream positions of science and history, they are more likely to dismiss this book's two-worlds thesis as parallel universe science fiction nonsense.

However, it is our contention that their weaknesses lie espe-cially in the problems they bring into their doctrine of Scripture and the nature of God's fairness, in order to hold to their position. We contend that such problems are sufficiently acute that their position is at least as implausible as ours, for those who accept a high view of Scripture.

Their key weaknesses, then, include these: Firstly, they have to accept that full theological humans, made in God's image, co-existed and likely interbred with mere biological humans, who were not in God's image. So, they need to explain the fairness of placing people in such a morally complex situation, from God's perspective.

Furthermore, their best route to retaining a high view of Scripture is to embrace a view concerning Genesis 1–11 that posits that God's word resides not in the literal descriptions of the events but in the interpretations of preexisting stories. Consequently, they encounter the challenge that, by their own standards, they cannot definitively discern which parts of the Genesis 1–11 stories consti-tute God's word, as they lack access to the comparative documents or oral sources necessary for making that determination. This means, according to their perspective, we cannot ascertain which elements of the Genesis 1–11 stories actually occurred.

Moreover, they are compelled to reject the notion that the genealogical data provided in Genesis 5 and 11 can be used to con-struct a timeline. This is despite Genesis containing precisely the data required for such calculations, and despite the lack of a viable alternative explanation for the age data other than representing the actual ages of the individuals in question.

Additionally, their perspective fails to explain and embrace many details of the scriptural text as well as our perspective does. Examples of these details include the change of behavior in *all* animals after the flood, the nature of recorded ages of the patri-archs in the generations after the flood compared with before, the conversation of Jacob with Pharoah, the fact of Cain receiving a curse on the ground in addition to Adam's curse, and the focus within the flood narrative on the specific date on which the flood occurred. Moreover, without incorporating this book's thesis regarding nations, those with a proto-historical-style view of Genesis 1–11 have great difficulty explaining what the historical events might be behind Gen 10:32, "from these, the nations spread out over the earth after the flood." Similarly, it is very hard for them to locate a historical context for a language that was once spoken worldwide and subsequently scattered near Babel. They often fail to focus on that question, because according to their viewpoint, such a scenario is impossible.

Our contention is that the collective weight of all these weaknesses means that this book's proposal is at least as plausible as theirs, even given our own speculations, both biblical and scientific. It is a significant *comparative* strength that this book provides viable historical proposals for understanding the context of Eden, the flood, the spread of nations, and Babel. It is a significant *comparative* strength that this book provides backing to embrace the historical creation of Adam out of dust and Eve from his rib, as well as the notion that a timeline can be calculated from the genealogies of Genesis, as well as a doctrine of Scripture that is not left dependent on the contents of ahistorical myths from long ago to which we have limited access. We contend that these strengths at least make up for perceived weaknesses that our thesis strays too much into the realm of parallel universe science fiction nonsense, or that it is too bold about what the most advanced prehumans could do without actually being full theological humans.

COMPARATIVE PLAUSIBILITY: LESS COMPREHENSIVE APPROACHES

After exploring these two approaches, which aim to harmonize the Bible's origin stories with our world while upholding a high view of Scripture, it is worth briefly mentioning some less-comprehensive approaches before we conclude. We could also have delved into the perspective that the Scriptures do not intend for Adam to be regarded as a historical figure. However, we find the biblical arguments supporting that position to be rather weak, and they have been addressed by other writers. Thus, we will conclude by briefly discussing the following approaches, which, despite their limitations, are prevalent enough to warrant mention.

The first approach was discussed in chapter 4, particularly concerning the flood. This approach involves noting that the phrase "all the earth" is used in Gen 41:57 to describe the eastern Mediterranean seaboard, rather than the entire globe. Some argue from this observation that the Bible may not be claiming a worldwide flood or making assertions about the global spread of nations and languages in Genesis 10–11, since the extent of what was understood to be "all the earth" back then was different from today's understanding.

However, this perspective faces a fundamental challenge that it does not provide sufficient explanation for many of the specifics of Genesis 1–11. In particular, it does not clarify whether the text implies that the mountains of Ararat were submerged while the rest of the world wasn't. It does not address the question of why Noah needed to save all species of animals if the flood account was intended to be read as a localized flood. It does not explain how all nations originated from Noah's descendants or how the Lord confused the language of the entire world at Babel, if this is the case. Thus, this approach does not offer a comprehensive framework for understanding Genesis 1–11 in relation to our world.

The second, less comprehensive approach to these questions is to say that it doesn't really matter how we integrate the teachings of Genesis 1–11 with the teachings of mainstream science and history. Especially with regard to Adam's creation, Cain's banishment, the flood, and the Tower of Babel, proponents of this position might say, "It is the meaning, not the fact, that we should focus on. The historical facts behind these stories don't really matter."

The issue with this perspective is that it essentially conveys that we cannot provide the meaning of significant sections of Genesis. For example, concerning the flood, proponents are essentially saying, "I cannot explain what it signifies when God declares his intention to wipe out all living creatures and the earth."

So, this stance suggests that we are unable to explain the meaning of a significant portion of the Bible, and that we should be fine with that. In response, one might envision Jesus admonishing Bible teachers who defend such a lack of understanding, by saying, "You are the teachers of the church, and yet you do not understand these things?"[1]

CONCLUSION

In sum, this book has examined the key segments of the Genesis 1–11 narrative, with a specific focus on those that present challenges when aligning with the timeline of origins established by mainstream science and history. Plausible understandings have been provided throughout that require neither the abandonment of mainstream science nor the abandonment of a high view of Scripture. This was achieved while holding to dates, derived in the traditional way, calculated from data in the Genesis genealogies. So, we have provided understandings of the historical character of events like the creation of Adam and Eve, the flood, and the Tower of Babel scattering. We have done so without the need to undermine the authority of the *descriptions* of Genesis 1–11. More than that, we have shown how the proposals of this book are not only plausible in their own right, but at least as plausible as the most comprehensive, most popular alternative views that come from a high view of Scripture.

Even for those who cannot accept all the details of these chapters, it is this author's hope and prayer that this work will serve to open the way for reengagement with Christianity for some of those 34 percent who presently feel blocked because of the Bible's position on science and evolution. It is also our hope that Christian preachers, parents, Sunday school teachers, and others might be helped by this book in expounding and applying the teaching of Genesis 1–11. May the glory go to God as we keep wrestling with his word and applying it to our lives.

---

1. See John 3:10.

Appendix

Calculating the Timeline's Key Dates

IN USING THE BIBLE to calculate a timeline of human origins, some important decisions must be made. The most important decision is the choice of text family, the LXX or the MT, to supply the "begetting ages" of the patriarchs. Also important is whether to include the lifespan of Cainan, who is included in the LXX in Gen 11:13–14 but not in the MT, whether the length of time the Israelites spent in Egypt was 215 years or 430 years, and whether the time between the exodus and Solomon's temple was 480 years or approximately 300 years. Each of these issues is complicated, but none of the choices fundamentally affects the arguments of this book. So, the explanations for the positions we have taken have been relegated to this appendix.

THE AGE DATA: LXX OR MT?

A choice must be made between the LXX and MT witnesses to the begetting ages of the patriarchs in Genesis 5 and 11. Regarding most of the patriarchs mentioned in Genesis 5 and 11, there is a difference of 100 years between the two witnesses, with the LXX providing a higher age than the MT. So, for example, a translation based on the MT of Gen 5:15–17 reads, "When Mahalalel had lived 65 years, he became the father of Jared. After he became the father of Jared, Mahalalel lived 830 years and had other sons and daughters. Altogether, Mahalalel lived a total of 895 years, and then he died." But a translation of the same passage based on the LXX reads, "When Mahalalel had lived 165 years, he became the father of Jared. After he became the father of Jared, Mahalalel lived 730 years and had other sons and daughters. Altogether, Mahalalel lived a total of 895 years, and then he died." The total years Mahalalel lived is the same in the two variants, but the age at which he became the father of Jared is 100 years higher in the LXX version.

The number of patriarchs with variants in their begetting ages is such that the MT/LXX decision makes around 1,550 years of difference for the date of the creation of Adam, and around 950 years for the date of the great flood. To consider the arguments in detail, Henry B. Smith's 2018 article is an important resource, and he does well both in outlining the issues, and in writing persuasively in favor of the LXX's witness.

The decision to make is whether to conclude that the LXX has *inflated* the numbers, or alternatively, that the MT has *deflated* the numbers. To grasp one of the more important arguments, note that while the LXX has a 100-year higher begetting age for each of the patriarchs, from Adam to Enoch and from Arphaxad to Serug, it is only *50 years higher* in the case of Nahor. Now, if the LXX had been inflating each of these numbers by 100 years from the pre-existing MT numbers, Nahor's age at the birth of his son could easily have been inflated from 29 to 129 years. Thus, it is hard to explain, under this hypothesis, why there was only a 50-year inflation in the case of Nahor. But this difference is easily explained if we suppose that the MT was deflating the begetting age years from the LXX original. Nahor is the only man in the Genesis 5 and 11 who in the LXX has a begetting age of his son less than 100 years. So, because his begetting age in the LXX was 79, a deflation of 100 years was not possible, which explains why a deflation of only 50 years was chosen, to yield the MT's figure of 29 years for Nahor at the birth of his son, Terah. This points to the likelihood that the MT deflation hypothesis is correct.

Additionally, in favor of the deflation hypothesis, is the observation that before Noah, there are three cases where the begetting age is the same in both the LXX and the MT. These are Jared, Methuselah, and Lamech. If the MT numbers were original, all three of these begetting age numbers could have been inflated by 100 years without problem. However, if the LXX numbers were original, Methuselah and Lamech's begetting age cannot be lowered by 100 years, for in that case they would outlive the flood. So, the deflation hypothesis explains the changes in a way the inflation hypothesis cannot, supporting the LXX as original.

Finally, again in favor of the LXX witness, is that early external citations of Genesis 5 and 11 reflect LXX testimony over against the MT, with relevant examples including Demetrius the Chronographer (c. 220 BC), Eupolemus (c. 160 BC), Pseudo-Philo's *Liber Antiquitatum Biblicarum* (first century AD), and Josephus (c. 94 AD). The only witness outside the MT that supports its figures is found within the book of Jubilees, which Smith argues persuasively is the erroneous source for the MT's shorter chronology.

WHETHER TO INCLUDE CAINAN IN GEN 11:13–14

The LXX of Gen 11:13b–14b includes the following, which serves to describe a patriarch named Cainan, who is not mentioned in the MT: "When Cainan had lived 130 years, he became the father of Shelah. And after he became the father of Shelah, Cainan lived 330 years and had other sons and daughters." So, the LXX has placed Cainan between Arphaxad and Shelah. Luke's Gospel follows the LXX, also listing Cainan between Arphaxad and Shelah in Luke 3:36. This is considered original by the editors of *The Greek New Testament*.

Smith argues persuasively for Cainan's originality in Gen 11:13b–14b, and against those who posit a scribal error in an early version of Luke's Gospel, pointing out that "Christian scribes across the Mediterranean world almost universally accept his name as original to Luke." He goes on to argue against the theory of Lukan scribal error. The unlikelihood of this theory can be seen in simply examining what is required to hold this position:

> According to this theory, Christian scribes also added Kainan to all known Septuagint (LXX) manuscripts of Gen 11:13b–14b dated prior to the 12th century AD . . . They also added Kainan to some manuscripts of LXX Gen 10:24 and 1 Chronicles 1:18, 24. Additionally, Christian scribes also amended extant copies of the pseudepigraphical *Book of Jubilees* by fabricating a biography for Kainan in chapter eight and inserting it between the lives of Arphachshad and Shelah.

It is more plausible to conclude that none of these proposed alterations were made by these scribes, but that the scribes in question faithfully copied the inclusion of Cainan, whose name was originally present in the relevant texts. So then, it is best to assume that Cainan formed part of the original text of Gen 11:13b–14, which adds 130 years to the chronology when compared to the MT version.

THE SHORTER OR LONGER STAY IN EGYPT

The main question regarding the length of the Israelite stay in Egypt regards how to integrate three key biblical texts. Genesis 15:13 tells us, "Then the Lord said to him, 'Know for certain that for *four hundred years* your descendants will be strangers in a country not their own and that they will be enslaved and ill-treated there.'" Genesis 15:16 tells us, "*In the fourth generation* your descendants will come back here, for the sin of the Amorites has not yet reached its full measure." Exodus 12:40–41 says, "Now the length of time the Israelite people lived in Egypt was 430 years. At the end of the 430 years, to the very day, all the Lord's divisions left Egypt." Note that LXX and Samaritan Pentateuch both contain an alternate reading of verse 40, saying, "the length of time the Israelite people lived in Egypt *and Canaan* was 430 years."

While some have argued that these chronological markers cannot be reconciled, this is not the case. It is best to conclude, with Glen Fritz,[1] that the 430 years of Exodus 12 stretched from the time Abraham was given the covenant, at age 75, to the time of the escape from Egypt, which is to say that it included both time in Egypt *and time in Canaan*. Regarding the time in Canaan, we may conclude that there were 215 years from the time Abraham received the covenant, at age 75, to the time Jacob entered Egypt. This includes the 25 years before Isaac was born, when Abraham was 100, the 60 years at which age Isaac became the father of Jacob, and the 130 years Jacob had attained when he entered Egypt, totaling 215 years. This leaves the remaining 215 years as the time the Israelites spent in Egypt, making a total of 430 years, as Exod 12:40–41 and also Gal 3:17 stipulate. This is to say that the alternate reading of Exod 12:40, "Egypt *and Canaan*," is the one accepted in this book's chronology, together with the 215-year stay in Egypt, rather than the 430-year stay.

The four generations mentioned in Gen 15:16 may be counted from Levi, as Kohath, Amram, Aaron, and Eleazar, the last of whom died in Canaan. One explanation for why the length of life is recorded for Levi, Kohath, and Amram in Exod 6:14–25, but not for any of the other men in that genealogy, is that these records draw attention to the four generations that fulfill the promise to Abram in Gen 15:16. That is, including the extended lifespans of 137 years attained by Levi, 133 years by Kohath, and 137 years attained by Amram serves to underline the reality that four generations was enough to span the 215-year stay in Egypt.

THE TIME BETWEEN THE EXODUS AND SOLOMON'S TEMPLE

There has been a long-running scholarly debate over the date of the exodus. The first major option that embraces a high view of Scripture is the traditional date of 1446 BC. This date is obtained

1. Fritz, "Sojourn in Egypt," 1–2.

by adding the 480 years of 1 Kgs 6:1 to the date of the dedication of Solomon's temple in 966 BC, which in turn is a multiply attested secure date. First Kings 6:1 tells us, "In the four hundred and eightieth year after the Israelites came out of Egypt, in the fourth year of Solomon's reign over Israel, in the month of Ziv, the second month, he began to build the temple of the Lord."

While an exodus date of 1446 BC is possible, we have chosen instead the chronology advocated by Kenneth Kitchen, supported more recently by Egyptologist James Hoffmeier. This chronology dates the exodus at around 1270–1260 BC. The major strengths of this chronology include that it allows Rameses, the place mentioned in Exod 1:11, to correspond with the city of Pi-Ramesses, built by Ramesses II, whose dates of rule were 1279–1213 BC. A second strength is expressed by Kitchen this way, as a problem with the early date: "the form of the Sinai covenant . . . excludes . . . any date of origin . . . before 1400/1360. Only with Suppiluliuma (ca. 1360–1320) . . . did this format come into use. So, a Moses in Sinai in 1447 could never have seen a format still to be invented half a century into the future!"[2]

In accepting such arguments for a late date of the exodus, it is necessary to embrace the notion that the figure of 480 years might be a symbolic one, deriving from 12 times 40. To this end, it is noteworthy that the figure "40 years" occurs with great frequency in the biblical chronology, especially in the period of the judges. It is also noteworthy that when the years explicitly mentioned between the temple dedication in 1 Kgs 6:1 and the wilderness wanderings of Num 14:33 are summed, the total adds up to considerably more than 480 years—633 years as enumerated by Hoffmeier. The statistical improbability of so many judgeships extending for precisely 40 years, combined with the complexity introduced by the overlap of different periods of judging, is enough to indicate that the symbolic use of the 40-year periods is possible, a possibility that can be embraced in order to dovetail better with the known history of Egypt.

2. Kitchen, *On the Reliability of the Old Testament*, 308–9.

TIMELINE OF THE PATRIARCHS

With this work done, we are in a position to present our timeline for the time of the patriarchs. There are other smaller decisions that we have made but not explained, such as the choice to follow James Ussher in taking Abraham to be born in the 130th year of Terah's life, rather than employ the 70 years mentioned in Gen 11:26, which we take to indicate Terah's age at the birth of his older brother. In the following table, in the places where decisions must be made about textual variants, we have followed quite closely the decisions of Smith in his article, "The Case for the Septuagint's Chronology in Genesis 5 and 11."

Name/event	Year BC widest possible range (earliest birth–latest death)	Year BC Best estimate birth	Year BC best estimate death	Age at death (LXX figures)	Age at birth of son (LXX figures)
Formation of our Earth		4.54 billion y.a			
First migration of indigenous ancestors to Australia	50,000–70,000 y.a.	65,000 y.a.			
Adam	5600–2700	5159	4229	930	230
Seth	5400–2600	4929	4017	912	205
Enosh	5200–2500	4724	3819	905	190
Kenan	5000–2450	4534	3624	910	170
Mahalalel	4800–2400	4364	3469	895	165
Jared	4700–2200	4199	3237	962	162
Enoch	4500–2700	4037	3672	365	165
Methuselah	4300–2000	3872	2903	969	187
Lamech	4100–2000	3685	2908	777	182
Noah	4000–1700	3503	2553	950	502
Shem	3500–1500	3001	2401	600	100
The flood	3000–2000	2903			

Name/event	Year BC widest possible range (earliest birth–latest death)	Year BC Best estimate birth	Year BC best estimate death	Age at death (LXX figures)	Age at birth of son (LXX figures)
Arphaxad	3310–1600	2901	2336	565	135
Cainan	3180–1600	2766	2306	460	130
Shelah	3050–1590	2636	2103	533	130
Eber	2920–1530	2506	2002	504	134
Reign of Ur-Nammu, ziggurat tower-builder	2168–2000	2112–2096			
Peleg	2780–1720	2372	2033	339	130
Reu	2650–1690	2242	1903	339	132
Serug	2520–1670	2110	1780	330	130
Nahor	2390–1720	1980	1772	208	79
Terah	2310–1630	1901	1696	205	130
Abraham	2180–1590	1771	1596	175	100
Isaac	2080–1490	1671	1491	180	60
Jacob	2020–1460	1611	1464	147	91
Joseph	1930–1410	1520	1410	110	

DATING THE BIRTH OF ABRAHAM FROM THE DATE OF THE CONSTRUCTION OF THE TEMPLE

In calculating the dates for the timeline, a key part of the process is to start with the date of the construction of the temple, known to have occurred in 966 BC, and from there to work back to the date of the birth of Abraham. The following table sets out important parts of the calculation and some relevant Scriptures.

Event	Years spent	Year BC	Relevant Scripture and Calculation
Abraham was alive but not yet in Canaan	75	1771–1696	Abraham 75 years old "when he set out from Harran," Gen 12:4–5.
Abraham, Isaac, Jacob were in Canaan	215	1696–1481	215 years = 25 before Isaac born Gen 21:5 + 60 years before Jacob born Gen 25:6 + 130 years, Jacob's age when he entered Egypt, Gen 47:9.
Israel was in Egypt	215	1481–1266	215+215 = 430. LXX and SP: Israel were in Egypt and Canaan for 430 years "to the very day" Exod 12:40–41. "the law, introduced 430 years later," Gal 3:17.
The time after the exodus	300	1266–966	"480th year after the Israelites came out of Egypt," 1 Ki 6:1. 480 taken as symbolic 12 times 40, representing around 300 actual years.
Solomon's temple construction begins		966	

THE FOUR GENERATIONS IN EGYPT AND THE WILDERNESS

In Gen 15:16, Abram is told, "in the fourth generation, your descendants will come back here." The following table sets out a way to count these generations. The table provides the age attained by each relevant patriarch, where available, as well as some scriptures demonstrating important details: that the first generation was in Egypt, that the last generation entered the promised land, and that each of those in between was the son of the one before, so that the table spans four generations. Kohath can be considered to be the first generation, since he was among those who "went to Egypt," making Elezar the fourth generation. Levi has been included, since some might argue that the first generation comprises all those born *between* Levi and Kohath, rather than simply considering that one patriarch stands for one generation. Either way, since both Levi and Kohath entered Egypt, it can be seen that the descendants of Abram returned from Egypt to the promised land in the fourth generation.

Name of Patriarch	Age Attained and Other Details	Relevant Scriptures
Levi	Entered Egypt with his brothers. Died aged 137 years.	Gen 46:8–11, Exod 6:16
Kohath	Entered Egypt with his Father Levi. Died in Egypt, aged 133 years.	Gen 46:11, Exod 6:18
Amram	Was born in Egypt, the son of Kohath. Died aged 137 years, most likely still in Egypt.	Exod 6:18, 20
Aaron	Was born in Egypt, the son of Amram. Died just outside the promised land, aged 123 years.	Exod 6:20, Num 33:39
Eleazar	The son of Aaron, likely born in Egypt. Served under Joshua in the promised land, age at death unknown.	Exod 6:23, Josh 14:1

Bibliography

Aland, Barbara, Kurt Aland, Johannes Karavidopoulos, Carlo M. Martini, and Bruce Metzger, eds. *The Greek New Testament.* 5th rev. ed. Stuttgart: Deutsche Bibelgesellschaft, 2014.

Alexander, T. Desmond. "Genesis Study Notes." In *ESV Study Bible,* 49–137. Wheaton, IL: Crossway, 2008.

Alster, B. "An Aspect of 'Enmerkar and the Lord of Aratta.'" *Revue d'assyriologie et d'archéologie Orientale* 67 (1973) 101–9.

Alter, Robert. *The Hebrew Bible: A Translation with Commentary.* Vol. 1. 3 vols. New York: Norton, 2019.

Augustine of Hippo. *The City of God (De Civitate Dei).* Vol. 1. Edinburgh: John Grant, 1909.

Austin, Steven A. *Grand Canyon: Monument to Catastrophe.* El Cajon, CA: Institute for Creation Research, 1994.

Bauckham, Richard J. *Jude, 2 Peter.* Waco, TX: Word, 1983.

Berkhof, Louis. *Systematic Theology.* Grand Rapids: Eerdmans, 1996.

Brinkman, J. A. "Appendix: Mesopotamian Chronology of the Historical Period." In *Ancient Mesopotamia: Portrait of a Dead Civilization,* 335–48. Chicago: University of Chicago Press, 1977. https://doi.org/10.7208/9780226177670-13.

Brueggemann, Walter. *Genesis: Interpretation: A Bible Commentary for Teaching and Preaching.* Atlanta: John Knox, 1982.

Calvin, John. *A Commentary on Genesis.* London: Banner of Truth Trust, 1965.
———. *Institutes of the Christian Religion.* Edited by John McNeill. Translated by Ford Lewis Battles. Philadelphia: Westminster, 1960.

Clarkson, C., Z. Jacobs, B Marwick, R. Fullagar, L. Wallis, M. Smith, R. Roberts, et al. "Human Occupation of Australia by 65,000 Years Ago." *Nature* 547:7663 (2017) 306–10.

Craig, William Lane. *In Quest of the Historical Adam: A Biblical and Scientific Exploration.* Grand Rapids: Eerdmans, 2021.

Dalrymple, Brent G. "The Age of the Earth in the Twentieth Century: A Problem (Mostly) Solved." In *The Age of the Earth: From 4004 BC to AD 2002*, edited by C. L. E. Lewis and S. J. Knell, 190:205–21. Bath: Geological Society of London, 2001.

Dawkins, Richard. *The Greatest Show on Earth: The Evidence for Evolution*. London: Transworld, 2009.

Driver, S. R. *The Book of Exodus in the Revised Version*. Cambridge: Cambridge University Press, 1911.

Dumbrell, William J. *The Faith of Israel: Its Expression in the Books of the Old Testament*. Leicester, England: Inter-Varsity, 1989.

Enns, Peter. *The Evolution of Adam: What the Bible Does and Doesn't Say About Human Origins*. Grand Rapids: Brazos, 2012.

Fritz, Glen. "The Length of the Israelite Sojourn in Egypt," 2016. https://ancientexodus.com/wp-content/uploads/2016/05/The-Length-of-the-Sojourn-in-Egypt_Glen-Fritz-160504.pdf.

Green, Michael. *The Second Epistle General of Peter and the General Epistle of Jude: An Introduction and Commentary*. 2nd ed. Leicester, England: Inter-Varsity, 1987.

Green, William. "Primeval Chronology." *Bibliotheca Sacra* 47 (1890) 285–303.

Grudem, Wayne. "Theistic Evolution Undermines Twelve Creation Events and Several Crucial Christian Doctrines." In *Theistic Evolution: A Scientific, Philosophical and Theological Critique*, edited by J. P. Moreland, Stephen C. Meyer, Christopher Shaw, Ann K. Gauger, and Wayne Grudem, 783–837. Wheaton, IL: Crossway, 2017.

Haarsma, Deborah. "A Flawed Mirror: A Response to the Book 'Theistic Evolution.'" BioLogos, 2018. https://biologos.org/articles/a-flawed-mirror-a-response-to-the-book-theistic-evolution.

Hamilton, Victor P. *The Book of Genesis: Chapters 1–17*. Grand Rapids: Eerdmans, 1990.

———. *Handbook on the Pentateuch: Genesis, Exodus, Leviticus, Numbers, Deuteronomy*. 2nd ed. Grand Rapids: Baker Academic, 2005.

Harari, Yuval Noah. *Sapiens: A Brief History of Humankind*. London: Vintage, 2015.

Hoffmeier, James K. "What Is the Biblical Date for the Exodus? A Response to Bryant Wood." *Journal of the Evangelical Theological Society* 50:2 (2007) 225–47.

Humphrey, Louise, and Chris Stringer. *Our Human Story*. London: National History Museum, 2022.

Kemp, Kenneth W. "Science, Theology and Monogenesis." *American Catholic Philosophical Quarterly* 85 (2011) 217–36.

Kidner, Derek. *Genesis: An Introduction and Commentary*. London: Tyndale, 1967.

Kitchen, K. A. *On the Reliability of the Old Testament*. Grand Rapids: Eerdmans, 2003.

Kramer, S. N. "The 'Babel of Tongues': A Sumerian Version" *Journal of the American Oriental Society* 88 (1968) 108–11.

BIBLIOGRAPHY

La Peyrère, Isaac. *Prae-Adamitae Sive Exercitatio Super Versibus Duodecimo: Decimotertio et Decimoquarto Capitis Quinti Epistolae D. Pauli Ad Romanos: Quibus Inducuntur Primi Homines Ante Adamum Conditi.* Amsterdam: Elzivir, 1655.

Layton, Scott C. "Remarks on the Canaanite Origin of Eve." *Catholic Biblical Quarterly* 59:1 (1997) 22–32.

Lefebvre, Michael. "Adam Reigns in Eden: Genesis and the Origins of Kingship." *Bulletin of Ecclesial Theology* 5:2 (2018) 25–57.

Longman, Tremper, III. *Genesis.* The Story of God Bible Commentary. New York: HarperCollins Religious, 2016.

Longman, Tremper, III, and John H. Walton. *The Lost World of the Flood: Mythology, Theology, and the Deluge Debate.* Downers Grove, IL: IVP Academic, 2018.

Lowery, Daniel D. *Toward a Poetics of Genesis 1–11: Reading Genesis 4:17–22 in Its Near Eastern Context.* Bulletin for Biblical Research 7. Winona Lake, IN: Eisenbrauns, 2013.

Mattessich, Richard. "The Oldest Writings, and Inventory Tags of Egypt." *Accounting Historians Journal* 29:1 (2002) 195–208.

McCrindle, Mark. "Faith and Belief in Australia: A National Study on Religion, Spirituality and Worldview Trends." McCrindle Research, 2017. https://mccrindle.com.au/wp-content/uploads/2018/04/Faith-and-Belief-in-Australia-Report_McCrindle_2017.pdf.

Merrill, E. "Chronology." In *Dictionary of the Old Testament Pentateuch*, edited by T. Alexander and D. Baker. Leicester, England: Inter-Varsity, 2003.

Morris, Henry Madison, and John C. Whitcomb. *The Genesis Flood: The Biblical Record and Its Scientific Implications.* Philadelphia: Presbyterian & Reformed, 1961.

Moshier, Stephen O. "Geology Does Not Support a Worldwide Flood." In *The Lost World of the Flood: Mythology, Theology, and the Deluge Debate*, 150–61. Downers Grove, IL: IVP Academic, 2018.

Numbers, R. "'The Most Important Biblical Discovery of Our Time': William Henry Green and the Demise of Ussher's Chronology." *Church History* 69:2 (2000) 257–76.

Patton, Matthew H., and Frederic Clarke Putnam. *Basics of Hebrew Discourse: A Guide to Working with Hebrew Prose and Poetry.* Grand Rapids: Zondervan Academic, 2019.

Poebel, A. "The Name of Elam in Sumerian, Akkadian and Hebrew." *American Journal of Semitic Languages and Literatures* 48:1 (1931) 20–26.

Quenstedt, John Andrew. *Theologia Didactico-Polemica.* 2 vols. Wittenberg: Quenstedt and Schumacherus, 1685.

Roux, Georges. *Ancient Iraq.* 3rd ed. London: Penguin, 1992.

Russell, Michael D. *Seeing Good, Doing Evil: The Limits of Moral Ignorance.* Eugene, OR: Wipf & Stock, 2020.

Sexton, Jeremy. "Evangelicalism's Search for Chronological Gaps in Genesis 5 and 11: A Historical, Hermeneutical, and Linguistic Critique." *Journal of the Evangelical Theological Society* 61:1 (2018) 5–25.

Smith, Henry B., Jr. "The Case for the Septuagint's Chronology in Genesis 5 and 11." *The Proceedings of the International Conference on Creationism* 8:48 (2018) 117–32.

Smith, Henry B., Jr., and Kris J. Udd. "On the Authenticity of Kainan, Son of Arpachshad." *Detroit Baptist Seminary Journal* 24 (2019) 119–54.

Snelling, Andrew A. *Earth's Catastrophic Past: Geology, Creation and the Flood.* Dallas: Institute for Creation Research, 2009.

Swamidass, S. Joshua. *The Genealogical Adam & Eve: The Surprising Science of Universal Ancestry.* Downers Grove, IL: IVP Academic, 2019.

Tattersall, Ian. *Becoming Human: Evolution and Human Uniqueness.* New York: Harcourt, Brace, 1998.

Turretin, Francis. *Institutes of Elenctic Theology.* Edited by James T. Jr. Dennison. Translated by George Musgrave Giger. 3 vols. Phillipsburg, NJ: Presbyterian & Reformed, 1997.

Ussher, James. *The Annals of the World.* Green Forest, AZ: Master, 2006.

Waltke, Bruce K., and Cathi J. Fredricks. *Genesis: A Commentary.* Grand Rapids: Zondervan, 2001.

Walton, J. H. "Exodus, Date of." In *Dictionary of the Old Testament Pentateuch*, edited by T. Desmond Alexander and David W. Baker, 258–72. Downers Grove, IL: InterVarsity, 2003.

Walton, John H. "A Historical Adam: Archetypal Creation View." In *Four Views on the Historical Adam*, 89–118. Grand Rapids: Zondervan, 2013.

Waters, Guy Prentiss. "Theistic Evolution Is Incompatible with the Teachings of the New Testament." In *Theistic Evolution: A Scientific, Philosophical and Theological Critique*, 879–926. Wheaton, IL: Crossway, 2017.

Wenham, Gordon J. *Genesis 1–15.* Waco, TX: Word, 1987.

Wilson, Robert R. *Genealogy and History in the Biblical World.* New Haven, CT: Yale University Press, 1977.

www.ingramcontent.com/pod-product-compliance
Lightning Source LLC
Chambersburg PA
CBHW060312100426
42812CB00003B/753